CHASING MY TAIL

CHASING MY TAIL

a memoir

EARL RUSSELL

iUniverse LLC
Bloomington

CHASING MY TAIL
A MEMOIR

Copyright © 2013 Earl Russell

iUniverse books may be ordered through booksellers or by contacting:

iUniverse
1663 Liberty Drive
Bloomington, IN 47403
www.iuniverse.com
1-800-Authors (1-800-288-4677)

ISBN: 978-1-4759-9650-0 (sc)
ISBN: 978-1-4759-9651-7 (hc)
ISBN: 978-1-4759-9652-4 (e)

Library of Congress Control Number: 2013911426

Printed in the United States of America

iUniverse rev. date: 6/25/2013

For
Kevin and Jason

TABLE OF CONTENTS

PREFACE

Just down the street from our house in central Georgia, a creek ran for about half a mile and spilled into the Oconee River. The creek was knee-deep and about ten feet wide. My friends and I spent many carefree days playing in the stream and swimming in the river.

When I Was a Boy

Growing up in the South was so much fun, with my dog, a fishing pole, cool streams, and the sun.

In the summer I'd go barefoot and shirtless too, and play in the woods with nothing else to do.

I'd go to the river and build a raft and dream of sailing on my sturdy craft.

I'd build my raft from fallen pines and lash them together with hanging vines.

With my dog as my first mate and me in command, we sailed down the river to a far-off land.

When we finally reached those distant shores, I would hurryhome to do my chores.

When I was a boy, I had so much fun, playing all summer under the Georgia sun.

This is the story of my life as accurately as I can recall. Some of the names have been changed simply because I can't remember all the names of the many people that are a part of this story.

This story is about happiness and sorrow, accomplishment and failure, pride and shame. I will attempt to tell it all for my children and their children so they will know something of me and what my life was all about.

In over twenty years traveling around the world from one side of the earth to the other, back and forth, back and forth so many times, it was almost like a dog chasing its tail. I suppose that's what I've been doing all these years—just chasing my tail.

ACKNOWLEDGMENT

A very special thanks to Mike Schultze for his book cover illustration of Earl beginning his journey.

INTRODUCTION

In writing these stories of my life, I start with Earl the teenager because I really can't remember the events of my early childhood.

As I move on through life I will write about the highlights of events that I remember most because if I attempted to write about my life in its entirety, I wouldn't have enough time left to finish the book.

The journey travels through time with a boy who survived rejection and despair and with wit and determination enlisted in the army as a sixteen-year-old boy. After extensive training I will fight in the Korean War. After leaving the army confused and without family or home, I will go on to the air force and remain until retirement.

Time after time I will volunteer for overseas duty and either live in or visit thirty-six countries and have many adventures, some good and some bad.

I will marry twice and have two sons and finally retire in Georgia, where it all started.

The stories will tell you about a boy, then about a soldier and finally about an old man.

I have lived a full life and experienced more than most men could experience in two lifetimes. I have no excuses for my many failures and no regrets for taking the risk that led to those failures.

The war in Korea was touched on lightly because it is impossible to describe what takes place in battle. The panic, the fear, the chaos, the sounds, the gore, and the smell of cordite are impossible to describe. All the men who participate in a single battle will tell a different story because they can't describe the battle we were in. It wouldn't be truthful; it would only be a confused afterthought.

I never panicked in combat because I was a soldier doing what I was trained to do. When the adrenaline subsided and the battle was over, sometimes I would weep. I'm not ashamed of that!

With all the hardships endured in the army, I still loved the army much more than the air force, and not a day goes by that I don't think of my fallen buddies.

So I will go through life in these stories and try to tell it like it was.

EARL

The year was 1937—the year my mother died. She was only thirty-nine.

At the time of my mother's death, I was two; my sister, Betty, was five, and my brother, Irvin, was eleven. I had two other siblings, Dub and Lucile. Dub was a nickname for W. H. Russell Jr. He was called W. H., but in the South *w* is pronounced "dubya," and that's why he got the nickname Dub. Both he and Lucile were married and didn't live with us at the time my mother died. Because they didn't live with us, they weren't affected in the same way the three of us were.

My father drank heavily after my mother was gone and couldn't or wouldn't take care of us anymore. So the decision was made to send us away to live with foster parents, Wallace Butts and his wife, Annie, (my mother's sister) in Milledgeville, a small town about thirty miles northeast of Macon in the center of Georgia.

Earl Russell

I believe my father was a weak man, because how could he abandon his children and allow us to be sent away? I didn't get to know him until years later, and even then, I didn't really know him because he wouldn't say anything personal about the past. Getting him to talk about himself was like getting water from a rock. Maybe he was ashamed.

MILLEDGEVILLE

Our new home in Milledgeville was totally different from our home in Macon. There was a big house with a barn and storage buildings, fenced-in pastures with cows, and horses. There were also chickens and ducks. When I was a little older, my daily chores were to milk the cows every morning and every evening. I also had to feed the chickens, and in the winter I chopped the wood for heating.

My uncle didn't care what I did as long as I did my chores. Aunt Annie and Uncle Wallace were in their midfifties when Irvin, Betty, and I went to live with them. They were already taking care of my father's oldest sister, Aunt Katie, who was mentally retarded to a small degree. She was small, with jet black hair that was always very neat and tied in a bun at the back of her head. She was always very kind to everyone. Taking in three young children must have been a tremendous burden on them.

Uncle Wallace was a hard-working man who almost always wore kaki pants with suspenders and a fedora style hat.

He wasn't very tall but was stocky and almost totally bald except for a little hair around his ears, and he constantly smoked a pipe.

When I was a toddler he called me "Dutch" because he couldn't understand what I was talking about. Later, when I was a little older, he would take me with him almost everywhere he was working. He was like a father until I got older, and then he grew more distant. He used to tutor some of the college students in math, but he would never help me with my homework. I really struggled in high school math, and, as a result, I still hate algebra.

Aunt Annie was a matronly looking lady who also wore her hair in a neat bun at the back or her head. She was a wonderful cook and seamstress and was always making quilts and comforters to sell and always seemed to have people waiting to buy them.

Aunt Annie was the disciplinarian, and while Uncle Wallace would swat me with his razor strap on occasion, she was much worse. Sometimes when I was late coming home to do my chores, she would make me go outside and cut a "switch" and bring it to her. If it wasn't big enough, she would keep making me go out until I brought her back one that was big enough to suit her. Then she beat me with the switch on my legs and back and sometimes drew blood. It wasn't always like that, and I don't mean to make it sound like she was a demon or something, but looking back on my childhood, I don't ever remember her giving me a hug.

She was adamant about us going to church and Sunday school and even Bible school in the summers. We all went to church three times a week, but I don't know if that made me a better person.

Every boy should experience growing up in a small southern town like I did. It was kind of a Huckleberry Finn lifestyle with many happy adventures and some not so happy adventures—some of which could easily land me in jail or maybe even prison in today's society. I'll get back to some of those adventures later.

I've already said why I came to this little town, so now I'll tell why I went away.

On a very hot day in July 1949, my uncle had assigned me to a job that would be very tough on a grown man, not to mention a boy of fifteen.

Uncle Wallace was a contractor who did all kinds of construction work, such as building bridges, moving houses, demolishing old buildings to make room for new construction, and all kinds of things like that. He had recently torn down an old warehouse and planned to reuse the bricks for new construction. The bricks were in large piles in a field behind our house, where they were to be cleaned and stacked onto a big flatbed truck. My job was to chip off the old cement and stack the cleaned bricks on the truck. The bricks were so hot from the sun that it was almost impossible to hold them without gloves, and I didn't have gloves. When I couldn't stand it any longer, I went into the house to try and cool off and figure out the best way to get the job done when in walked Uncle Wallace. I was standing in the kitchen drinking a glass of water with no shirt on and sweat dripping down my face and body when he yelled, "What are you doing in the house?!" I replied that I was just trying to cool off a little. That's when I heard the words that still echo in my mind, after all these years. "Put out or get out!" Those were the last words I heard from his mouth for several years. He went out the back door, and I went out the front door with the clothes I had on and without a penny in my pocket. It was the last time I ever set foot in that house.

He was the only father I ever knew, and I loved him like a father. Until that day I thought he loved me too. It wasn't because of an adolescent rebellion that I left; it was the pain of being totally rejected by him.

His wife (my Aunt Annie) had died a few months before, and he had recently remarried. I didn't like his new wife very much, and I could tell that she resented my being around. I guess that had something to do with his change of attitude. I don't know.

I was only fifteen years old when those words, "Put out or get out," changed the course of my life. He put a lot of emphasis on the words "get out," so there was no mistaking what he meant. He slammed his fist on the table, and, pointing at the door, he shouted the "get out" part!

THE JOURNEY BEGINS

On the way out of the house I stopped in the bedroom long enough to grab a pillowcase and stuff in a pair of pants, a shirt, and shoes.

I can't imagine anything more devastating to a boy of fifteen than to suddenly find himself homeless, without a dime in his pocket, and only the clothes on his back, not knowing where his next meal was coming from or where he would find shelter. Those shouted words, "get out," would ring in my ears for the rest of my life.

I was in such a state of despair that my head was spinning, and I had no idea where I was going or what I was going to do. I walked aimlessly for a long time, and that night I slept under a bridge on dry sand next to a creek. I was hungry, tired, and confused. I cried myself to sleep.

When morning came I washed in the creek and walked to the highway leading out of town toward Macon. I had decided to go to my sister Lucile's home and make a plan with her help.

I thumbed rides until I finally reached Macon. Not knowing where to go, I found her street address in a phone book and kept asking directions and walking until I found her house. I must have walked twenty miles that day. I couldn't call to let her know I was coming because I had no money, not even a dime for the phone call.

When I arrived at her door she was totally shocked to see me. I didn't know until then what she looked like because I don't remember ever seeing her. I too was surprised to learn that my brother, Irvin, was living with her and her husband, Hugh.

I learned after a few days that I couldn't stay there either, so it was off again to places unknown. My brother offered to go with me to Dub's (my other brother's) home in a little town in Alabama called Red Level (population five hundred), so the next day we got on a Greyhound bus for the trip to Red Level. After we arrived we were greeted by Dub and his wife, Louise, at the little house they had rented near an old factory building. Dub had bought the building and converted it into a factory, where he designed and manufactured office furniture.

After a couple of days Irvin went back to Macon, and I remained with Dub and Louise for a few more days. I was told by Dub that I couldn't stay there because he didn't have the time or the money, and he didn't want the responsibility. Louise wanted me to stay and finish high school in Red Level, but Dub said no.

Dub bought me a train ticket and told me to go to Memphis, Tennessee, and find my father. So off I went again with my father's last known address and nothing else.

MEMPHIS

The train ride to Memphis gave me plenty of time to think. There were very few passengers, so I had my choice of seats. I looked out the window at the passing countryside and ate the sandwiches that Louise had made for me. She also gave me a small piece of luggage for my one pair of pants and one shirt. I got rid of the pillowcase that I had been using. At least now I didn't look so much like a hobo while carrying that pillowcase.

Finally the train arrived at the Memphis terminal, and I set off on the search for my father. I knew the street name and address, so I kept walking and asking directions as I went. As I walked down the Main Street toward Linden Avenue (the street I was looking for), I was a little afraid and overwhelmed at the size and sights of this huge city. At least I thought it was huge at the time. But a few years later Memphis would seem small in comparison to the cities I would visit. New York, London, Frankfurt, Munich, Tokyo, Hong Kong, and Bangkok, just to name a few, were awaiting my destiny.

When I finally reached Linden Avenue, I walked about a mile until I reached the address I was looking for. My father wasn't there, and he didn't live there. I went to a phone booth and tried to find him in the book, but obviously he didn't have a phone, so I couldn't find him.

Now I was down to my last sandwich, and it was night again. I had no place to go, and I was very tired. I decided to go back to the train station and at least be inside for the night, so I walked the three or four miles back.

The next morning I washed in the men's room and retraced the path I had taken yesterday. I went past Linden Avenue and turned down Beale Street. Beale Street in the 1940s and 1950s was a dirty street teeming with undesirable people, not at all like the tourist attraction it is today. It was mostly black clubs, bars, and pawn shops, and almost no white people. Dub had given me a few dollars, so I went into a hot dog-hamburger place and got a couple of hot dogs for a dime each. That's about all I lived on for the next couple of weeks except for two or three meals a very kind black man gave me.

At night I would alternate between the bus station and train station to sleep, and sometimes I would sleep in large cardboard boxes behind stores. During the day I would get my hot dogs and wander around trying to find a job of some kind to earn some money.

One day I was standing in the doorway of a club trying to keep dry because it had been raining all day, and I was wet and cold. A black man who owned the club came to the door and asked me what I was doing there. I explained that I had come from Georgia in search of my father, and I had been walking all over Memphis and couldn't find him anywhere. Then he asked if I had any place to stay, and I told him I was sleeping wherever I could find a safe, dry place. He went back inside the club but after awhile he came back outside and asked if I was hungry and took me inside and fed me. He said his name was Sam. He was tall and thin with almost white gray hair, and when he smiled, his eyes twinkled.

Since it was still raining, he offered to let me sleep on an army cot upstairs in a storage room. I accepted his offer, and that night I listened to the music downstairs until I went to sleep. All they played was blues music, and I still love it today. The next morning I swept out the club and cleaned the tabletops. He didn't ask me to do it, but I felt obligated to do something for his kindness. I don't know why a black man would be so compassionate to a white boy during that time in the Deep South, but I will always be grateful.

In a few days I would be sixteen, and I was in serious trouble. With no money and no place to live, I was at a dead end.

During the following days I spent all my time looking for a job. I had to have money. At last, I got a job at a company that made furniture. The name of the factory was Cole Manufacturing Company, and my pay was seventy-five cents an hour. Wow, thirty bucks a week.

I found a boarding house within walking distance of my job at twelve dollars a week. I got one meal a day, a bed, and a shared bathroom. Now I had enough money to buy some more clothes and some more food.

The job at the factory wasn't very hard compared to what I was used to working for my uncle in Milledgeville. All I had to do was keep the workstations supplied with material to be assembled and keep the floors swept up around the saws and drill presses. I kept busy, so the days went by fast. When the factory whistle blew, I would punch out on the time clock and go back to my little room at the boarding house, clean up, and have my meal with the other boarders. The meal was usually stew or chicken and dumplings and always included biscuits and plenty of vegetables. This was the routine for several months.

I knew I had to do something to change the direction my life had taken; I hadn't finished high school, and there was no way I could go back to school now. So I paid a visit to the Armed Services Recruiting Center.

When I went into the center, recruiters from each branch of the service were at desks lined up side by side. I wanted the navy, but the recruiter said, "Come back next month, because our quota is full." So I went to the next desk for the army. The sergeant said, "Sit down, son." He asked my age, and, although I had just turned sixteen, I told him I was seventeen. He gave me a parental consent form, told me to get it signed and notarized and bring it back with my birth certificate. Now I had another problem—no parent and no birth certificate.

I went to the county health office to find out how I could get a birth certificate. They gave me the address of the health office in Macon, where I was born. I wrote to them, and in a few days I received a form to be filled out and notice of the fee required. By the time I got the birth certificate it was March. The certificate wasn't a true birth certificate, but a certification with the date of my birth typed in numbers instead of words. I solved my age problem by going to a store and getting some ink remover. I very carefully removed the 8 (August), and then I went to a pawn shop on Beale Street. The owner let me use one of the pawned typewriters for a charge of fifty cents or a quarter; I don't remember which. With the simple stroke of my finger, I was now seventeen years old. I had changed the 8 to a 1 (January). I made the "new" birth certificate look old and worn. Now all I had to do was get the parental consent form signed and notarized.

An old man who was always hanging out around the bars and liquor store near my boarding house appeared to be about the age of my father. I gave him a couple of dollars, and he agreed to go to a notary with me and sign my father's name and get the paper notarized. Done!

The following Monday I went back to the army recruiter with my required documents. They gave me some test and told me to come back the following morning for a physical exam. I passed all the tests and was scheduled a couple of days later to be sworn in with a group of other guys. On the way back to the boarding house I stopped by to say good-bye to Sam at his club. When we shook hands, his big hand almost swallowed up my little, skinny hand. He said good-bye with that deep voice of his and that twinkle in his eyes. I have always regretted not keeping in touch with my friend.

Me in front of boarding House (age 15)

THE ARMY

We were sworn in by a captain, who congratulated us and promptly turned us over to a sergeant. He said in a loud voice, "Men, you are now the property of the US Army. If any of you decide to go over the hill, the FBI will bring you back, and you will be in deep shit." Nobody went over the hill, and we all showed up at 0800 the next morning for the bus ride to Fort Jackson, South Carolina. For the first time in over a year I felt safe and secure. I had found a home, the US Army.

Over the previous few months, I had thought a lot about Milledgeville and the friends I left behind. There was Frank, who was my best friend, and L. K., Bookie, Harold, Junior, Wendell, and so many more that I would miss a lot. I would also miss the military school where I was a cadet and where I played football. The school was Georgia Military College, with grades six through junior college. I had been going to GMC, as it was known, for almost five years and knew a lot about the army's drills, ceremonies, and the M1 rifle. I could drill with the best of them and disassemble and reassemble the M1 rifle with ease. Now that I was in the army I was sure glad I had gone to military school. It gave me a jump start and the ability to adjust quickly.

Before boarding the bus to Fort Jackson, our tough-talking sergeant asked, "Is there anyone here with military experience?" Without thinking, I held up my hand and said yes. He said, "Okay, Russell, you're in charge until the bus gets into Fort Jackson." "Crap," I thought. "I had to open my big mouth." Most of these guys were draftees and were much older than me, and now everyone was looking at me as if I was a snake.

The bus ride to Fort Jackson was uneventful. I didn't have to do or say anything as the "man in charge." All I had to do was carry all the record jackets of the new inductees to whomever relieved me when we arrived. I guess I looked less like a snake now that we were off the bus, because I no longer got those "looks." It was probably my imagination anyway. But it did teach me to keep my mouth shut.

We were assigned to a barracks, given sheets and blankets, and told to make our bunks and stand by. I made mine with hospital corners the military way and stretched the blanket tight enough for a quarter to bounce. Most of the guys didn't do so well, and their bunks looked pretty bad, but that was okay, because we weren't in training yet.

All we had to eat during the long bus ride was boxed lunches, so now we went to the mess hall and had a meal before sacking out for the night.

The next day it was raining and dark outside when a sergeant woke us up by beating on an empty trash can and yelling for us to get out of the sack. "Get up. Get up. Drop your cock and grab your socks. Get up. Get up!" After breakfast at the mess hall we drilled in the rain. None of us had rain gear, and it was cold. It was the first part of April, and even in South Carolina it's still a little cool. By the time we finished drilling in the rain and mud, we all looked like drowned rats.

The next morning, I was making my bunk and passed out. I woke up on the floor with one of the guys kicking my feet and saying, "You can't fake your way out of any details by doing that." After I got on my feet, I got permission to go to sick call at the clinic. It turned out that I had a fever, so the doctor gave me some medicine and a light duty slip, and I spent the rest of the day in the barracks.

The next day we were loaded onto a troop train for a long ride to Fort Hood, Texas. This would be the second time riding on a train as a passenger since leaving Milledgeville. Frank and I used to jump on freight trains and ride in the boxcars for miles and then jump off and walk for miles down the tracks back to town—not smart but fun. Another thing we did that wasn't too smart was to go out on the railroad trestle over the river and play a game to see who could hold on the longest. The trestle was about a mile long without a walkway along the track. A bunch of us would go out on the trestle over the river and wait for a train to come along. Then we would go under the tracks and hold on to the cross ties while the train passed overhead. Sometimes the train would be very long and moving kind of slow, so when we couldn't hold on any longer, we would simply turn loose and drop about a hundred feet into the river. Then we would swim ashore and laugh! It was great fun but a little dangerous.

Another thing that was fun on hot summer evenings was to climb up the ladder of a water tank and go for a swim. The tank was one of those big open-top water tanks next to the railroad tracks, which were used to fill up the boilers on the steam locomotives.

When we spotted a night watchman, we would be very quiet until he went away. Then we would climb back down the ladder and go away. It was a lot of fun, and we never did get caught.

Now I was about to do something else that could be very dangerous. I was on a troop train on the way to Fort Hood to train for war. Thousands of soldiers were being trained for the Korean War, and I would be one of them. For some reason I wasn't afraid; I even looked forward to being a good soldier and doing whatever I was trained to do.

The train took a couple of days to get there, and we even had bunks where we slept in Pullman cars. To pass time, most of the guys would play cards or roll dice. When the train went through New Orleans, it was going about as fast as a person could walk, so some of the men would jump off, run to a liquor store near the tracks, and then jump back on. I didn't drink or gamble, so all I did was talk to some of the guys and look out the window. I had never traveled anywhere before leaving Milledgeville, and now I had been to Alabama, Tennessee, South Carolina, Louisiana, Mississippi, and soon Texas. Later in my life

Earl Russell

I would visit all fifty states and thirty-six countries. At mealtime on the train, instead of boxed lunches, we had C rations. I had heard how bad they were, but they really were not that bad. At least they filled the hole in my stomach. We finally reached Fort Hood, and we all got a little nervous with anticipation of things to come.

Remembering

I became a cadet at Georgia Military College at the age of thirteen, in the eighth grade. In those days, GMC was a true military academy run by a commandant who was an active-duty army lieutenant colonel. Each morning a bugle call would announce the uniform of the day, and our daily activity would be governed by strict military practices and a code of conduct. It was one of the best military schools in the South, from which top cadets would go on to West Point or the Naval Academy.

In later years the school turned coed and even allowed some students to wear civilian clothes. It is no longer the respected military school that it once was.

By going to GMC I had learned a lot of the army's regulations, drills, ceremonies, and protocol that would put me way ahead of most army recruits and help me to hit the ground running when I signed up.

At the school I participated in most sports—football,

baseball, basketball, and boxing. I loved football and boxing, but I gave up basketball because I was always getting ejected from games. When some tall, lanky, bony player would poke me in the face with his elbow, I would knock the crap out of him and get thrown out of the game.

My dream was to finish school at GMC and go to the University of Georgia and play football for the Bulldogs, but my dreams were never to become reality.

When I wasn't going to school I had to work for my uncle at his construction projects. I would drive trucks and do labor along with a lot of the black workers he had. When he moved houses, he would build wooden tracks under the house and use the rollers made up from cut sections of telephone pole about five feet long. As the house would be pulled slowly by tractors, the rollers had to be repositioned quickly as they rolled out the rear. He had me under those houses when I was twelve and thirteen years old, an extremely dangerous job. If the house had fallen, I would have been nothing but a greasy spot and a memory.

Once when he was doing some work on a bridge for the state, he used Georgia chain gang prisoners to do labor. I worked along with the prisoners, and I talked with them a lot. Most of the prisoners weren't bad men, just unlucky.

Once someone dropped a very expensive drill bit into about fifteen feet of water and nobody could get it out. I said, "I'll get it," and dove in and came up with the bit. I was the hero of the moment. It was a very hot day, and the water was cold and, oh, so nice.

My uncle wasn't all work and no play because he allowed me to be active in the Boy Scouts. I never became an Eagle Scout, but I came close. I eventually wound up with nineteen merit badges of the required twenty-one. I was also an Explorer Scout and Order of the Arrow. An Order of the Arrow candidate is chosen by his peers and must pass some rigorous tests. I was led into the woods blindfolded at the end of a rope and turned loose to spend the night without a sleeping bag, food, or anything else. The next morning I would locate the other two or three candidates, and we would build a little bridge over a creek without a spoken word. The only tools we had were our scout knives. It wasn't easy.

I got into some trouble as a boy, too. The city had given permission for my scout troop to build a small, one-room scout hut on a city property. We put in a lot of work and finally finished the project. The city then decided to let all the scout troops have the hut. That made us mad because it was so unfair. We solved the problem! I stole a stick of dynamite from my uncle's construction supplies, inserted a cap and fuse, and blew the dammed thing off the map.

It didn't take a very smart person to figure out where the explosives came from. I had to stand in front of Judge Bell, a friend of my uncle, and be chewed out and preached to, along with the other boys. We didn't admit anything, and nobody could prove we did it, but when I went home my uncle beat me pretty good with his razor strap.

Another time I almost killed a kid and was very lucky I didn't. I was walking home from roller skating around the loading docks at the railroad station and had my skate straps buckled together and hanging around my neck. The skates were steel with those little hooks that attached to your shoe soles.

Along came William Landry, a guy much bigger than me, and he said, "Hey, you son of a bitch!" I said, "What did you say?" He repeated it. I said, "You called my mother a dog?" He said, "Yes, she's a bitch." At that I grabbed one skate and swung the other one around like I was doing a hammer throw and hit him so hard on the side of his head that it knocked him off his feet. He was out cold and lay on the ground with his legs twitching and his eyes rolled back. A lady came running out of her house screaming, "You killed him; you killed him!" Well, I didn't kill him, but you can bet your ass that when he saw me coming after that, he went the other way. I got off with a warning when my uncle learned why I did it. I think he was kind of proud of me. I had gained a reputation of being a badass, but I really wasn't; I just didn't take any crap from bigger kids, that's all.

A bunch of us kids were having a marshmallow roast and drinking hot chocolate in Sonny Goldsten's back yard when the funniest thing I have ever seen happened. We were using straightened coat hangers to roast our marshmallows over an open fire. A girl with long blonde hair, almost down to her waist, very pretty and very stuck-up, was in the yard along with about a dozen kids. My marshmallow caught fire, so I just flipped my coat hanger, and the flaming marshmallow went flying though the air like a meteor and hit directly on top of pretty little Brenda's perfect blonde hair. Her hair caught fire, and one of the kids started beating her on the head. My friend Roy got so tickled that he squirted hot chocolate out his nose. Thinking he was choking, another kid started beating him on the back. Sonny's mother came screaming off the back porch, and I just stood there and put another marshmallow on my hanger wire. Nobody knew where the meteor had come from. It was the funniest thing I ever saw. Even today, every time I think about it, I can't help but laugh.

FORT HOOD, TEXAS

A long line of trucks was waiting for us when the train stopped at Fort Hood. We were all given our assignments and told which truck to get on. My assigned unit was the 701st Armored Infantry Battalion, Headquarters Company.

When we arrived at our company area, we were assigned to barracks and claimed our bunks. They were all double bunks, and I chose the top. After we left the barracks, we were taken to the barber shop, where we lost all, and I do mean all, of our civilian hair. After the haircut, we were issued uniforms and given instructions on arranging our footlockers and hangers. Then we would go to our mess hall for a hot meal. Each company had its own mess hall, which could feed over 150 men. Later on the army would do away with individual mess halls for each company and consolidate into one very large mess hall that could feed thousands. The cost savings to the army must have been tremendous.

The next few months at Fort Hood were going to be hell, but we still found time to have a little fun and laugh.

So many men were lost because of inadequate training at the beginning of the Korean War, and for that reason our training had been extended. We had eight weeks of basic training and eight weeks of advanced training.

The first day was low-key and easy, but that was not to last.

The next morning we woke up to a screaming, whistle-blowing, trash-can-beating, cussing sergeant. It seemed like all these guys used the same phrase: drop your cock and grab your socks. I think they make all the noise to see if anyone is going to have a heart attack, so they can get rid of the weak ones. Not really, but it seemed that way.

We had about five minutes to pee, splash some cold water on our faces, and get dressed. We didn't have to worry about combing our hair. We didn't have any.

Now our loudmouth sergeant was in front of the barracks blowing his whistle and yelling, "Fall in. Fall in." The whole company was now on the company street forming into platoon formations. There were four platoons with four squads of nine men in each platoon. After some more screaming and cussing, we went back into the barracks and made our bunks, shaved (I didn't have to shave), and went back outside, where we got back into formation and went single file into the mess hall.

After breakfast, the instruction would start that would gradually form us into soldiers.

A couple of days later our platoon sergeant asked if anyone had any military training, and this time when I said yes, I was made a squad leader and given a white armband with corporal strips.

After a few days, we were issued M1 rifles with serial numbers that we had to memorize. On paydays we would have to salute the pay officer, give our name, rank, serial number, and rifle number before we would receive our pay.

One day while we were learning to disassemble, assemble, and properly care for the weapon, one not so bright soldier screwed up big-time. We had the rifles disassembled and all the parts spread out on our ponchos (rain gear). One of the parts was a gas cylinder rod, which is a little over a foot long and hollow with a slight curve to it. The not so bright soldier thought it was bent and tried to straiten it out. He ruined it and had to pay for the rifle, the cost of which was a little over seventy dollars.

Soon we started our training on the firing range. We had to qualify with the M1 rifle from two hundred, three hundred, four hundred, and five hundred yards. I also had to qualify with the M1 and M2 carbine, .45-caliber pistol, .45-caliber submachine gun, and .30-caliber machine gun.

Toward the end of our first eight weeks, all the scores were posted on the company bulletin board, where I learned that

I had qualified along with the best marksmen in the army with the M1 rifle, the top 5 percent in the entire army.

During the eight weeks of advanced infantry training we would train with the .50-caliber machine gun; the BAR, or browning automatic rifle; bazooka; mortar; and .75 mm recoilless rifle.

Now that our basic training was over, we were given a couple of days off before hell would start again. To celebrate, some of us went to the beer garden and had a few beers. I had never drunk before in all of my sixteen years, and I was feeling it pretty good by the time we went back to the barracks. I was sitting on the rail of the fire escape balcony on the second floor talking with some of the guys when a guy from another platoon came out to join us. He was a Mexican American who was drafted, and all he wanted to do was bitch about the army and the USA. I called him a wetback son of a bitch, and he hit me in the mouth and knocked me off the rail. I fell to the ground below, but I wasn't hurt. I had the breath knocked out of me, and I had a bloody mouth. By the time I climbed the ladder back to the balcony, my buddies had beat the crap out of the Mexican. I never heard him complain after that.

When our little break was over, we woke up at 0200 to the sounds that we all had learned to hate.

I never had any problem getting up, because when I was growing up in Milledgeville, my uncle would call me once. If I didn't get up after he had called me that one time, he would throw the covers back and hit me a hard blow with his razor strap. It didn't take too long to learn to get up.

The reason for the early wake-up this time was a very bad announcement. We were going to break the battalion speed march record to north Fort Hood. It would be with full packs, rifle, and steel helmet. We were told to fill our canteens and carry extra socks and foot powder. We would have enough time to eat and be ready by 0400.

The distance to north Fort Hood was thirty miles, and we did break the battalion record. The bad news was that now we were going back to south Fort Hood and break our own record. We had a one-hour rest while we ate and took care of our feet. We started back and did break our own record. We had gone sixty miles. We lost a few guys to foot problems and other physical problems, but most of us came through okay.

After twenty-four hours to recuperate, we got back to our regular training.

I found myself in trouble one day while in class in a warehouse that we were using for weapons training. We had our ponchos on the floor and a disassembled BAR on the poncho. The guys were passing around a little eight-page pornographic comic book. When the book reached my poncho, wouldn't you know it, I was the one who got caught! The sergeant standing in back of the class suddenly smacked me on my helmet liner with his swagger stick, and the sound almost deafened me. The helmet liner is made of plastic and is used as a liner for the steel helmet that fits over it. The liner is used as normal headgear instead of a soft cap. The liners were spray painted and waxed until they were very shiny. Anyway, the sergeant took me to the commander, along with the comic book. No matter how I tried to explain that the comic book wasn't mine, it made no difference to the captain. He gave me an article 15, which is company punishment instead of a court-marshal and consists of two hours of extra duties each day for two weeks. The punishment doesn't go on your records, so when you ship out to another unit, you start out with a clean record.

My punishment was to dig a hole and bury the book and fill it back in. The hole was six feet deep, six feet long and six feet wide. This was to be done using my little entrenching tool, a folding shovel that is normally used for digging foxholes. The soil in Texas is hard and rocky, and it took me about ten days to complete. The rest of the time I spent marching with my field pack filled with rocks.

Another time I made a clumsy mistake but not serious enough for an article 15. The platoon was stacking weapons in preparation to leave them there for physical training exercise. When we were filing out of the formation, my foot hit the butt of a rifle and the stack fell on the ground. A squad will make three stacks with three rifles in each stack. The rifle has a little hook near the muzzle that is used to hook the rifles together to form a tripod of rifles. My punishment was to clean all three rifles and sleep with them under my covers that night. That wasn't fun. I wasn't the only soldier that got in trouble. Everyone did at one time or another.

The sixteen weeks of hell were finally over, and now we were full-fledged soldiers ready for combat if necessary.

Most of the company got orders for Korea or other places. I

was to stay at Fort Hood as a driver for S-1 Headquarters. I drove a jeep for a lieutenant colonel, and when I wasn't doing that, I stood guard duty or KP or whatever they could find for a private to do. The funny thing is, when I was assigned as a driver, I didn't even have a driver's license. They just asked me if I could drive, and I said yes. I'd been driving cars, trucks, and tractors for my uncle since I was twelve years old.

One weekend I went to Temple, Texas, about thirty miles away with a couple of guys, and when we went through the little town of Belton, I noticed a little airport with a sign: "Reed's Air Service." I didn't stay with the others and instead went back to the airport to find out about flying lessons. I started taking lessons with Pete Reed, a big, friendly Texan who I liked a lot. Before I left Texas I got my pilot's license.

Now that training was over, about all we were doing was sitting around thinking of things to do.

One night a lot of the guys went to a movie because it was raining, and there wasn't anything else to do. We didn't have television in those days, so about all we could do was play pool in the dayroom across from our barracks, play cards, or go to the beer garden. So, since it was raining and the movie would be over after lights-out in the barracks, I thought it would be fun to surprise our wet buddies when they came in the barracks door. The dayroom was a long building about twenty yards from the barracks, and since it was raining, everyone would run to the dayroom and walk through the dry room and make a mad dash back through the rain to the barracks door. We stacked a bunch

of footlockers that were painted olive drab (OD) in front
of the open door and formed a wall about four or five feet
in front of the door. You guessed it! A couple of guys came
flying across the walkway and crashed into the wall of
footlockers. They were mad as hell! It's lucky that nobody
got hurt.

It's really hot in Texas in August and September, and we
didn't have air conditioning or ceiling fans in the barracks.
So, needless to say, you would lie in your bunk and sweat.

I went over to the mess hall to see my friend, Jimmy the
cook. I got some confectioner's sugar from him and took
it back to the barracks. One of the guys who was always
playing jokes on us wasn't there at the time, so I pulled back
the sheets on his bunk and sprinkled the confectioner's
sugar on the bottom sheet and neatly made his bed.

It was really funny watching him roll over, and the sheets
sticking to his sweaty body. He didn't think it was funny
and wanted to kill someone. Nobody told him I was
the jokester. A few days later I told him, though, and he
laughed.

Another time I took a nylon shaving brush and snipped off
the ends of the bristles and sprinkled them on a guy's sheet.
The nylon was transparent and was like a thousand little
needles sticking him. He wanted to kill someone too, and,
again, nobody told on me.

Orders were coming down every day, and a lot of the guys
were being reassigned to armored units, where they would
be trained as tank crews. Orders were also coming down for

Korea. I didn't mind going to Korea, but I didn't want to be a tanker. Tanks were hot as hell in the summer and like ice in winter, and you were always covered with dust. I didn't want to take the chance of being a tanker, so I went to the orderly room and told the first sergeant that I wanted to go to ranger school. He arranged for my tests and physical and said, "Okay, you can go if you qualify."

I took a written test, which was actually an IQ test, and I passed both the test and the physical. I don't know if the written test was to see if you were smart enough to be a ranger or dumb enough. Anyway, I passed and was off to ranger school.

Before I left, Jimmy and I went to the Rattle Snake Inn one night about twenty miles from Fort Hood. It was the closest place to buy booze. I had won an old beat-up 1939 Ford in a crap game, so we drove that to the inn with no working gas gauge. We bought a gallon of cheap wine, drank about half, and headed back to the fort. After driving about halfway back, we ran out of gas. After a short discussion I decided that Jimmy was too drunk to walk down the road to look for gas, so I went. After about four or five miles of walking I came to a farmhouse. As I approached the house a dog came running out and bit my leg and ripped my pants; the farmer came out on his porch with a shotgun and yelled, "Who's there?" I identified myself, and he called off that crazy dog. I explained that I had run out of gas and wanted to buy a couple of gallons so I could get back to Fort Hood. He siphoned some gas out of a truck and gave it to me so I could get back to the car.

When I got to the car with my bloody leg and the can of

gas, Jimmy had ripped open my rear seat cover and was sleeping under it. I asked why the hell he did that, and he said, "I was cold!" We got back just in time for reveille, so we didn't get into trouble.

Basic Training (age 16)

Ranger School

I thought I was going to Fort Benning to ranger school, but my commander sent me to the First Armored Division's ranger school there at Fort Hood. At the time, I didn't even know the First Armored had a ranger school, but I was soon to find out the hard way. Major General Bruce Clark had formed a school at Fort Hood that would compare to the one at Fort Benning. General Clark was the best training officer the army had, and he would pay frequent visits while we were in training, to observe our progress.

The first morning we went on an early four-mile run before breakfast, to be followed by a four-mile run every morning. On Saturdays it was increased to a ten-mile run. Also, when we were outside a building, we were not allowed to walk; we had to run whenever we were not under a roof.

The training would consist of several elements and would last eight weeks. There would be tactics, survival, demolitions, repelling, weapons, hand-to-hand combat (martial arts) map reading, physical training, and more.

At the beginning of the school, we were a company of 150 men. Only eighty of us graduated, and of the eighty, I graduated thirtieth in my class. I was very proud of that. When I saluted General Clark and receive my diploma, I was on cloud nine and could hardly wait to go back to my company and show the captain and first sergeant what I had accomplished. I'm sure they thought I would drop out of ranger school and come back with my tail between my legs. Instead, I came back showing off my new ranger patch, the sign of a soldier's soldier.

After reuniting with my friend Jimmy, it would be off again for more training and counterfire school at Fort Benning. I gave the old Ford to Jimmy. Most of the guys that I knew had shipped out for Korea or other places, so it wasn't like home at Fort Hood any more.

At Fort Benning, I would train for what I would be doing in a combat unit in Korea. The counterfire training was actually sound ranging. Two teams would locate an enemy weapon by triangulating the sound of the weapon, locate it on the map, and call in the coordinates to artillery to fire on the target. The entire process would take about sixty seconds and was extremely accurate. The danger to the teams was that they had to be even with or in front of the friendly fire so as not to confuse the sounds. It was bad enough being on the line, but being all the way up front was scary as hell.

I had been in intense training for almost a year, and it seemed that I was the most well-trained soldier in the army. My training was over, and I got orders for Korea. I knew it was coming, and now it was here.

Shipping Out

When I left Fort Benning I was wearing a new stripe on my sleeve. I was now a PFC, or private first class.

On my way to Fort Lewis in Tacoma, Washington, where I would board a troopship for Korea, I decided to stop in Macon to visit my sister Betty and her husband, Mac, and then visit my older sister, Lucile, and brother, Irvin. I thought about going to Milledgeville too, but I didn't because I still had bad memories and didn't want to see my uncle again. Not yet anyway.

Growing up in Georgia and spending so much time on the river and camping in the woods really made survival training easy for me.

I had been very active in the Boy Scouts and Explorer Scouts, so living and surviving in the woods was more fun than anything else. My dog, Pal, and I would go down by the river and make a lean-to, where I would build a fire and fish. I would cook the fish and some corn that I "borrowed" from a farmer's field, and Pal and I would spend two or three days by the river, all this, of course, with my uncle's permission. One summer a group of Explorer Scouts were making a canoe trip down the river to earn a merit badge. The trip was 120 miles, and there were four canoes. A game warden went along with us just for the fun of it. He was an old man named Jerry Lowe, and he carried along a rifle. When it was time for some food, we stopped our canoes under some willow trees to eat in the shade. Mr. Lowe's canoe was near mine, and as he was eating, he suddenly said, "Don't move, boy." He pointed his rifle over my head, and there was no way I wasn't going to look to see what he was aiming at. He fired a shot, and a big cottonmouth moccasin fell into my canoe, and I jumped into the water. My canoe partner, Roy, then flipped the snake out and into the water, and I jumped back into the canoe. It all happened so fast that it must have been funny as hell to those looking on. Jerry Lowe always called me "River Rat" after that.

I cut my leave short and left Macon for Fort Lewis. I changed planes in Atlanta and again in Chicago. The plane I boarded in Chicago was the first double-deck aircraft to be used in commercial aviation. It was designated the Stratocruiser, and the military designation was the C-97. The air force also had a tanker, the KC-97. On the flight a couple of businessmen invited me to the lounge on the upper deck, and we played cards all the way to Seattle.

When I finally got to Fort Lewis and signed in, I was assigned a barracks with a bunk next to a window with a fantastic view of the snow-capped fourteen-thousand-foot Mount Rainier. It was beautiful, and I went up there with a buddy and his girlfriend and tried my skill at skiing which was really bad. I spent more time on my ass than I did on the skis.

I'm glad I spent a few days in Washington before we boarded the ship for Korea. It gave me some time to explore Seattle and the surrounding area.

One night when I was in Tacoma, I ran into a buddy with whom I took basic training. He was on his way home from Korea and had some real stories to tell. We talked about a lot of guys, and we wondered what had happened to one in particular, Eddy Fisher. Eddy was the singer who would later marry Elizabeth Taylor. He wasn't well liked by most of the guys, and he only took the first eight weeks of basic and was then reassigned to special services. We never heard from him again. I guess he was entertaining the troops someplace.

It was hard to believe that some of my buddies that I took basic training with were coming home after seeing combat in Korea. Some had been decorated for bravery and some had purple hearts for wounds received in combat. Now it was my turn.

THE TROOP SHIP

The USNS (US Naval Ship) *General McRay* was in dock waiting for us to board for the first leg of our voyage to Korea. The first stop would be Japan for a couple of days, then another ship to Korea.

I was one of the unlucky two hundred men selected for advance party. We would board a couple of hours before the remainder of the two thousand troops and three hundred officers would come aboard. At first I thought being on advance party was a good thing, but I soon found out that I would be working shift duty in the ships galley (kitchen). For the next fourteen days of the trip to Japan I would work six hours on duty and eighteen hours off. It really wasn't bad; we got to eat before the others, and we had better food. It would be the last time I did KP in the army.

The USNS *General McRay* was one of many built by Henry J. Kaiser to ship cargo and troops during World War II. Our sleeping quarters were canvas bunks stacked five high with enough room to barely turn over. If a big man was under you, he couldn't turn over without his shoulder nudging you in the back. I was advised by one of the crew that a lot of men would get seasick, so the top bunk would be the safest place to be to avoid being splashed by vomit. I took the top bunk among the steam pipes and electrical cables. It was tight, but I didn't get splashed.

We steamed out of Puget Sound in Seattle and out to sea for a two-week cruise to Japan. The trip was uneventful but interesting. We saw all kinds of sea life—whales, sharks, flying fish, you name it.

A big initiation ceremony was held when we crossed the international date line and, everyone received certificates.

Two black soldiers on board were acting like they were gay. They each had little blue ribbons in their hair and were really laying it on thick. In those days a homosexual would get kicked out of the army, and it was obvious that was exactly what they wanted. They didn't want to go into combat, and their intent was to be shipped back to the States and be discharged. A wise officer made them remove the ribbons and act like soldiers or spend the remainder of the trip in the brig.

About fifty miles from the coast of Japan a little white speck on the horizon kept getting bigger and bigger until it turned into one of the most beautiful sights I have ever seen. It was Mount Fuji—a snow-covered volcano—on the island of Honshu.

We finally docked in the port of Yokohama and boarded a train for a short ride to Camp Drake. Once there we were given a cot in a big warehouse of a barracks and a much-needed freshwater shower. The ship couldn't distill enough fresh water for so many men, so we had had to take saltwater showers for the past two weeks. The food at Camp Drake was much better than the ship's food, and it was also great to walk on solid ground again.

That night we went to a huge warehouse that had been converted into a beer hall, which had long tables with benches. All the guys at my table started building a pyramid with the empty cans, and when it was completed with the last can it seemed to explode! Someone at another table had thrown a full beer at our pyramid and hit it dead center. A fight broke out with about a hundred guys participating until the MPs stopped it and closed the beer hall. None of us were really that drunk on the 3.2 beer, but there are always some guys who get really stupid when they drink. Nobody got hurt in the brawl, only some black eyes and fat lips. I guess the tension was pretty high because everyone knew that in a few days they would probably be facing the real enemy in Korea.

The next morning we were given our field gear, helmets, and brand new M1 Garand rifles. The rifles were packed in cosmoline (a thick, waxy type of lubricant). After cleaning and oiling our new weapons, we went to the rifle range to fire and zero in the sights to get ready for action. The remainder of the day was spent reading mail and writing a letter home before boarding another ship for Korea early the next morning.

LOOKING BACK

It's odd, but I wasn't afraid at all. Instead, I was sad. I was eager to prove myself as a soldier, and I knew there was no way I would show any cowardice under fire. I sure hoped not, anyway.

I was sad because about all I could think about was Milledgeville and what was and what could have been.

Playing football at GMC was my first love, and my goal was to eventually play for the University of Georgia. My uncle Wallace had a son who was the head football coach at Georgia, and he was always telling me to do well at GMC, and I would someday play for him. Wally Butts was one of the best coaches in America, and until he took over as head coach, the university had never been to a bowl game. In twenty-two seasons his teams won 140 games, lost eighty-six and tied nine. He also went to eight bowls, and won four SEC titles and one national championship.

I don't know if I would have been good enough for first string, but at least I would have gotten an education.

My sister Betty was also on my mind. I remember walking to school with her when we were both in elementary school, and her little pet ducks trying to follow her to school. It's funny how you remember things like that in moments like this. I made my sister the beneficiary on my military life insurance policy, and had I been killed in Korea, she would have gotten $10,000. I don't know if I ever told her that.

My uncle also had a friend who was a very powerful congressman. Carl Vinson. He had a farm just outside Milledgeville, and one day when I was about seven or eight years old, I had a childhood illness, mumps, measles, or something like that, I don't know. Anyway, in walks Carl Vinson with my uncle into my bedroom. He was carrying a baby goat. He put the goat on my bed and said, "Get well, boy, so you can play with your goat." I named him Major, and he became a great pet. He followed me everywhere that I would allow him to. The navy later named a nuclear aircraft carrier after the congressman the USS *Carl Vinson*.

While I was at Fort Hood I had gotten a pilot's license and a driver's license and had passed my GED test in the top 10 percent of those tested in the United States that month. Later on I would attend evening classes at several colleges and universities but never got the degree that I wanted.

It was time for me to be a man now and stop looking back and start preparing for what lay ahead.

I was seventeen years old and was about to board another ship for the final leg of the trip to Korea.

KOREA

My new orders were to report to the Fifth Regimental Combat Team, one of the most highly decorated regiments in Korea. In fact, they had more battle streamers on their regimental flag than any other regiment in Korea. The Fifth RCT stands in the annals of military history among America's most storied regiments. As the soldier that I thought myself to be, it was an honor to be assigned to this fine fighting regiment.

The Fifth Regimental Combat Team was exactly that, a combat team. It was almost like a small division. It consisted of three infantry battalions, an artillery battalion, a tank battalion with about twenty tanks, an engineer company, a medical company, rangers, and now a counterfire platoon. The Fifth RCT was highly mobile and could pack up and redeploy very quickly. I'm talking about minutes not hours.

The troopship USNS *Marine Phoenix* was waiting for us

at the port of Yokohama for the final leg of our journey to Korea. It would take only two days to get there.

Again, we were packed in like sardines, but this time it wouldn't be so bad for only two days. We all carried our rifles and field gear, and this time we looked a little more like soldiers.

We sailed away across the Sea of Japan toward the southern coast of Korea.

When we got near the port at Pusan, we could smell Korea before we could see it. The farmers all used human feces for fertilizing their rice paddies, and the whole country smelled like one big outhouse. The Korean people were very poor in this war-torn country and didn't have chemical fertilizers, so they did what they could to raise their crops and survive. I could certainly understand it, but it still didn't help the smell any.

We off-loaded from the ship at Pusan and boarded a US Army operated train that would carry us north as far as the tracks went because the tracks had been destroyed before the train reached our destination.

When we boarded the train, each soldier was given one clip of ammo and ordered "not to load." One clip held eight rounds, not enough to do much good in a fight.

I was the highest-ranking soldier on my car with my one little stripe and was made the car commander. That was the first time I had ever been the commander of anything. As the train started north we were told not to take anything from the many civilian beggars that swarmed the train each time it slowed down to a near stop. The fear was booby traps, and we didn't want to lose any fingers or eyes.

Some of the men in my car were asking me many questions as though I was a seasoned combat veteran, and I told them I was as green as they were and didn't know a damn thing about what, where, when, or anything else. Many of the men were scared, and you could see it in their eyes as we passed destroyed towns and villages, and the farther we went the worse it got, but the smell didn't change.

When the train reached the Han River, just south of Seoul, we got off the train and loaded onto trucks to cross the river and drive through the city. It was sad to see such destruction of a once thriving city. Most of the buildings had been damaged pretty badly, and there weren't many people on the streets. Oddly, though, the queen's palace, which was pointed out to us by our truck driver, didn't seem to be damaged at all. I didn't even know South Korea had a queen.

We continued going north through the town of Uijonqbu, and near the town of Chunchon we stopped for the night and for some food with the Third Infantry. After eating some C rations we climbed into our fart sacks (sleeping bags) for some much-needed sleep.

The next morning we rolled up our fart sacks, had a hot meal, and loaded onto trucks for our final destination, the Fifth RCT.

We were being escorted by a second lieutenant and a

sergeant from the Fifth RCT. The lieutenant would be in our truck and the sergeant in the other truck. The lieutenant was very young, tall with blond hair, and appeared to be about twenty-two years old, probably fresh out of some college ROTC program. He must have been the low man on the totem pole to draw the assignment of escorting us to the Punch Bowl. The sergeant was older and probably had plenty of combat under his belt.

Only two trucks going to the Fifth RCT, and all the other men would be sent to units all over the place.

We finally got under way and drove for a few miles up the MSR (main supply route), the equivalent to a main highway. Along the MSR I saw a sign on the side of the road that read, "Caution, you are now under enemy observation." The sign didn't make me feel warm and fuzzy inside! The army engineers put signs up along the MSR in appropriate places to keep you alert.

Eventually we turned off the MSR onto a small secondary road and followed it to the end, where we would unload from the truck. I was glad that the ride was over, because the roads were very bumpy and after awhile the truck would have beaten us to death. The other truck had dropped back to keep from eating our dust. So far I didn't recall seeing any paved roads anywhere in Korea.

Now it was time to lock and load the one clip of ammo that we were given on the train in Pusan. We still hadn't been given any more ammo, but it didn't seem to be a big concern since we had been told that we would be in a "safe zone" until we reached the CP (command post) of the Fifth RCT at the Punch Bowl, where we were headed. There we would get more ammo before joining our platoons, which were in position on the face of the Punch Bowl.

About a dozen men were on our truck, and we would go first, followed by the second group a couple of minutes later. The path or trail, about a half mile long, zigzagged through rocky terrain leading up to the rim of the Punch Bowl. The lieutenant, who was as green as we were, was leading us up to the CP when we rounded a bend in the trail around some boulders, and all hell broke loose! An explosion right in front of the lieutenant took him down along with a couple of other guys. I don't know if it was a mortar round, artillery, or a grenade, but it caused panic and reflex in the men to turn around and run back down the trail to find cover. Four or five Chinese soldiers were waiting for that to happen, and the guys ran right into their fire. Luckily for me, I didn't run down the trail but instead dropped to the ground like a ton of bricks and tried to burrow myself into the ground like a mole, hoping that my backpack would provide some protection. Everyone was firing at the gooks, and the group coming up the trail behind us arrived just in time to help finish off the little commie bastards. A squad of men came down the trail when all the noise started to lend us some support, but by the time they reached us it was all over. I still had a couple of rounds left in my M1, and I don't even remember firing at the Chinese. I guess I didn't have time to be afraid while the firefight was going on, but when it was over, I was shaking like a leaf. The squad had come down to help lead the way up the trail to the CP.

We had lost two men, the young lieutenant and one of the new guys. Four guys were wounded; luckily I didn't have a scratch. I didn't know any of their names, but later I learned the lieutenant's name was Collette.

Everybody was mad as hell because this should never have happened. Somehow the Chinese had slipped through a hole in the line without being detected and got caught in the morning daylight and couldn't get back to their own line. Or at least that's what we thought. Someone was probably sleeping at his LP (listening post) and didn't see them.

When we finally reached the CP we were told by the regimental commander, Colonel Wheeler, that we shouldn't worry because we would be put with veterans. Some of them had only been on the MLR (main line of resistance) for twenty-four hours, but they were veterans. Hell! We hadn't even reached the MLR, yet and we were veterans! This was not a good way to start the day with a new outfit. That warm, fuzzy feeling was gone and wouldn't return to me for a very long time.

THE COUNTERFIRE PLATOON

When we got to the CP the sergeant who escorted us gave a report of what had happened on the trail, and all of us had to answer some questions about the incident. Somebody was going to be in big trouble because lives were lost due to neglect at one of the LPs.

When all the questioning was over, Corporal Jeffries came to the CP to take me to the counterfire platoon. I would share the bunker with Corporal Jeffries and a private first class named Cook, because the corporal wanted me to learn the ropes as quickly as possible. I was assigned to one of the teams as assistant squad leader. Later on I would gradually move up to squad leader of the Fourth Squad, then Third, Second, and finally squad leader of the First Squad with the rank of corporal. The First Squad leader was considered assistant platoon sergeant, but all this would take about three or four months as wounded or killed were taken away or guys rotated back to the States.

The job of the counterfire platoon was to take sound bearings on enemy targets and call in fire missions to artillery to take out the heavy weapons on those targets. The equipment was a recording devise about thirty inches long, ten inches wide, and ten inches thick supported on one end by bipods. It had an extendable eyepiece for viewing a scope (cathode ray tube) kind of like a very small TV screen. When the sound of a weapon was captured on the recorder, it would cause a little bright dot to bounce around on the scope until it was brought under control and into a straight horizontal line by manipulating a little thumb-controlled wheel. Numbers on each wheel were then put on a computing board and then on a plotting board. There were two teams about one hundred yards apart, and the recording devices of both teams were controlled by a telephone wire. When the sound was heard by the controller at team number one, a button was pressed that would stop each recorder and then both teams would get their readings at the same time. The numbers were called in to team number one, which would get the map coordinates then call in a fire mission to artillery. This whole procedure took about sixty seconds—not enough time for a big gun to be moved. The recordings were extremely accurate to within ten yards. At each team a triangle of three microphones was leveled and precisely positioned so that we could triangulate and locate the target. Three men would operate the device, radio, and equipment while about fifteen men would provide protection for each team with M1 rifles, BARs, and light machine guns. The really scary part for the counterfire platoon was that we had to be even with or in front of our own lines so as not to confuse the sounds. One of our guys would always be located at the 555th Field Artillery (Triple Nickel) to coordinate fire missions. We would rotate, and each time the duty at Triple

Nickel would last about a week. It would get us off the line for a while, and we welcomed the change.

The Punch Bowl was a nasty, godforsaken place that smelled of death and rotting flesh. It was two mountain ridges facing each other with a valley in between called no-man's-land. In no-man's-land were rolls and rolls of barbed wire that had dead Chinese tangled in the wire and rotting. The enemy couldn't get their dead because we would only kill more of them, so they just left them there. When the wind blew the wrong way, the smell was awful. Several attempts to cremate the bodies with napalm helped a lot.

The American side of the Punch Bowl was lined with sandbagged bunkers connected by trenches that went for miles.

Every day the Chinese would fire machine guns (MGs) at our positions or fire mortars or artillery. The fire would be sporadic, and you never knew when it was coming. The MG slugs would hit our sandbags with a thump before we heard the sound of the guns. I had a few close calls because I was careless but lucky.

Night was worse than daylight hours because we never knew when a patrol of Chinese would infiltrate and drop into our trenches and catch a soldier sleeping and cut his throat, which happened a couple of times. I would sleep with my hand under my head to keep my ear from being blocked from sound by whatever I was using as a pillow. I still sleep that way after more than fifty years. I guess the North Koreans and Chinese made a lasting impression on me!

In a foxhole or bunker there had to always be one guy awake, and there was absolutely no smoking after sundown. The enemy could either see the glow of the cigarette or smell the smoke, and that invited disaster. If you got caught smoking after dark, you may have gotten a rifle butt in the teeth, because you were putting your buddies at risk.

Firing tracers at night would piss me off too because if we could see where our fire was going, the enemy could see where it was coming from! They would only increase their firing to try to take out the gun doing the firing.

On one occasion some "very bright" officer had some big searchlights brought up to the MLR and set them up right by our bunkers. You don't have to be too smart to know what happened after dark when the lights were turned on and started shining on the enemy on the other side of no-man's-land. We started taking MG, mortar, and artillery like you wouldn't believe. The lights were never used again, but we took some casualties from that screwup. I wonder where the officer got his training.

One day when nothing was going on, I was lying on my fart sack in the bunker when all of a sudden ... Bang! I damn near died of heart failure, only to find out that Cook had shot a big rat with his M1. We had rats because so many guys didn't bury their C ration cans and just left the empties on the bunker floors or outside on the ground. The rats liked the treats. I told Cook that if he did that again, he may wind up just like the rat.

One day when it was quiet and no incoming fire had come in for a while, a tall, muscular private first class was standing outside the bunker when a mortar round exploded right by him. I looked up, and he was still standing there, but half of his jaw was gone, and I could see his teeth and tongue. There was no blood at first, but then it really started pouring. We did all we could until the medics took him away. He was a physical education instructor at a college in Ohio before joining the army. His name was Stevens, and we never saw him again.

You can imagine the emotional pain of seeing your buddies killed or wounded. I could never wish war on my sons or their children.

The counterfire platoon was attached directly to headquarters, so that we could get orders directly from the regimental commander, and was sent wherever we were needed the most. Consequently, we moved all along the MLR, and after being at the Punch Bowl for about two months we were to move again and help Triple Nickel Artillery take out enemy positions that was raising hell with some other elements of the Fifth RCT farther down the MLR.

A small river was nearby, and after digging in and setting up our equipment, three or four of us at a time would go the hundred yards or so to the river to take a bath for the first time in over a month. The water was ice cold and wonderful. God, it felt good to be clean!

I was now a corporal and squad leader of the Fourth Squad.

A few days before I had picked up an M2 carbine from an

unlucky soldier who wouldn't need it anymore and turned in my M1 to our supply sergeant. The M2 is fully automatic with a thirty-round magazine compared to eight rounds for the M1 Garand. I took two magazines and taped them together, one pointing up and the other pointing down. That gave me sixty rounds altogether. I could be firing one of the thirty-round magazines and loading the other so that when one was empty, I could quickly flip it over and insert the other so I could keep firing. The M2 carbine was the fastest-firing weapon the army had at the time and would fire at a rate of 720 rounds a minute compared to the .30-caliber machine gun at a rate of 550 rounds a minute. I kept the carbine the rest of the time I was in Korea.

Most attacks came during the hours of darkness, and on this particular night it would be bad. We had been hit heavily by artillery all during the day, and the wounded had been evacuated before nightfall. I guess the Chinese thought we would be exhausted and be sound asleep when they infiltrated around three or four in the morning. The enemy soldiers were probably platoon strength, and when the firing started, there was no mistake that it was enemy fire because their weapons sounded completely different from American weapons. It was a chilling thing to wake up to that sound. The fight seemed to last for hours, but it was probably more like thirty minutes. They were probably trying to take some prisoners but didn't succeed because when they were discovered and fired on, they were forced to fight instead.

Firing on a man at a distance is like shooting at a target. You can't see his face, so it is very impersonal. You squeezed off a round and saw him fall, so you knew it was a hit, but it didn't mean anything because it was only a target.

This time it would be different, though, because when I was running down the trench line, I came face to face with a Chinese soldier, who was running right at me with his weapon pointing in my direction. I fired a burst of six or seven rounds into his chest, and he just fell backward and sat on the ground with his back against the wall of the trench and looked at me while he died. He was probably about fourteen or fifteen years old. It's a terrible thing to look into the eyes of a soldier and watch him take his last breath. It affected me in such a gripping way that I started sobbing and didn't stop for a long time.

I don't think I ever knew how to pray, but after that night I talked to God a lot. I don't know if he listened, but I talked to him anyway. A strange transformation took place in me after that night, and I would feel invincible for the rest of my time in Korea. Maybe it was just that I didn't give a damn if I died or not.

We had killed eight of the enemy and taken a couple of prisoners. I don't know how many got away. We had some wounded, but no one was killed.

A few days later we pulled off the MLR and went into reserve for a couple of weeks to resupply, eat hot food, and sleep in cots in tents.

Taking a very cold bath

LIEUTENANT DAN

This time reserve would be different because we had a new platoon leader fresh from the States—Second Lieutenant Dan Martin. Dan and I had gone to the same military school in Milledgeville (GMC), and we had a lot to talk about. I liked Dan a lot, and he was a very sharp soldier.

For the next couple of weeks we would be having field exercises to bring Lieutenant Dan and our other replacements up to speed on the counterfire platoon's equipment and procedures. This time when we went back on the line, I would be assistant platoon sergeant as the squad leader of the First Squad. The title was in name only because I was only a corporal not a sergeant.

While we were in reserve one of the guys in the company went completely crazy and set up a .30-caliber machine gun and started shooting at anything and anybody who moved. Lieutenant Dan and I were lying in a ditch for cover while this nut was trying to take on the whole company! Lieutenant Dan told me to work my way close enough to take him out and stop his killing spree, and Dan would try to divert his attention away from me! I wasn't quite ready to be shot full of holes, and I told Lieutenant Dan, "Hell, no, you work your way in, and I'll keep his attention!" So while Lieutenant Dan and I were trying to decide who would do what one of the other guys shot him and silenced his machine gun. The reason I argued with my platoon leader is that I just didn't want to kill one of our own guys. I could have been in serious trouble by my refusal to obey an officer, but Lieutenant Dan let it go and forgot it. If it had been an enemy soldier, there would have been no hesitation doing what I was ordered to do. I'm lucky I didn't lose my stripes.

While we were in reserve hot meals were a daily luxury along with showers in a couple of tents that were set up along with big water tanker trucks. It was really great getting rid of about an inch of crusty grime from my body. We were even given two cans of beer each (opened, of course). It was "Lucky Lager" beer.

It had been a very hot summer, and now it was starting to get cool. I was not looking forward to the cold that would come in a couple of months.

Back on the MLR

The point system determined when a soldier would go home. Combat troops would get four points a month, support units three points, and nonsupport units two points. When thirty-six points were reached, I could go back to the States. I had been in Korea for six months and had accumulated twenty-four points with twelve more to go for a total of nine months of combat.

When we went back on the line it was in an area called the "Iron Triangle" near the thirty-eighth parallel, where heavy fighting had been constant for a long time. As always, the Fifth RCT was assigned to fill up the weak holes in the line. The Chinese and North Korean armies were really giving us hell with their artillery by day and small-arms fire day and night.

The counterfire platoon would set up our equipment on the line and try to locate and silence some of those big guns. We found a suitable location with two hills about two hundred yards apart. Perfect! The two teams would go into their positions from the back side of the hills so as not to be exposed to small-arms fire. The only problem was getting the communications wire from team A to team B. There was no way to get it there without being exposed. The guys were arguing about whose turn it was to take the roll of wire across the open area. All the while those guns were making a lot of noise, and that meant our guys were getting hurt or killed. The reel of wire is called a doughnut, which is attached to an A-frame backpack, and the wire feeds out by itself when the bearer walks or runs with it. While these guys were arguing I grabbed the pack and ran like hell across the opening. Not a shot was fired! I was lucky! I don't know if it was luck or insanity, but we got the equipment working and started locating the guns so our own artillery, "Triple Nickel," could take them out. Had I known the opening was mined, there is no way in hell I would have run through it! It wasn't bravery that made me take the action that I did; I was just pissed off that the guys were wasting time and doing nothing to locate those guns.

A couple of days later, Lieutenant Dan went down to "Triple Nickel" artillery to watch our counterfire coordinator work with the artillery guys and the platoon. The same day that the lieutenant had gone back to "arty," we were hit very hard and lost a couple of guys killed and a couple wounded, including our platoon sergeant. Now I was in charge of the platoon, and the first thing I did was change the position of our automatic weapons. If we were infiltrated, the gooks would try and take out our machine guns because they knew where they were. Not only did it change the positions, but it improved the field of fire so the entire area was covered.

As it turned out we were not infiltrated, and all went well until the following morning.

As was his custom, the regimental commander paid us a visit early that morning and looked over our area. I told him the platoon leader was down at artillery, and the platoon sergeant was evacuated late yesterday. When he asked me who was in charge, I told him I had assumed command since I was assistant platoon sergeant. The colonel gave me a "Well done" and said, "I'm promoting you to sergeant. Do you know why I'm promoting you?" I said "Yes, sir, because I'm a damned good soldier!" I wish I hadn't said that because it made me appear to be arrogant and cocky. Because I said it with a grin on my face, I suppose it was okay with him. He just smiled and walked away. I couldn't put on my new sergeant stripes until we went back in reserve because I didn't have any way to get stripes on the line. I was now one of the youngest sergeants in the army. I was still eighteen years old. My buddy Ernest Cook poked me in the stomach with his M1 rifle, threw the bolt back, and said, "Don't let those strips go to your head, Russell." I hope he had the safety on!

One of the funniest things that I saw on the MLR was the destruction of some of our piss tubes. During one of the attacks by the North Koreans they dropped hand grenades into some of the piss tubes that we had installed as urinals. For sanitation purposes we buried artillery canisters about a foot deep in the ground with about two feet sticking up out of the ground to be used as urinals. The canisters are used to transport the 105 mm artillery shells. The gooks thought they were chimneys for underground bunkers, and their grenades blasted urine all over the place, including all over them.

This time when we left the line, a very tragic thing happened that I still think about after all these years. We were in trucks going down a mountain road about four or five miles behind the line when one of the trucks ran off the road and crashed down the side of the mountain. Seven guys were killed in the accident. We lay them down along the roadside, face up, until a litter truck could come and take them away. The company commander said, "I need a volunteer to stay with these men until the truck gets here." I volunteered because these were my buddies, my friends. It was several hours until the truck arrived and way after dark. While I was waiting, some of the bodies would move slightly because of rigor mortis setting in. It was kind of creepy watching the bodies, some with their eyes still open. It was an awful experience but something I felt I had to do.

When I got back to reserves with my platoon, it was time to go on R & R in Japan. R & R stands for rest and recreation. It would be a nice break to get away from the war. We had lost most of our platoon due to killed, wounded, or rotation back to the States.

I was going to Kokura, Japan, on the southernmost Island of Kyushu.

When I was getting ready to leave the platoon some of the guys asked me to bring them back something. You would think they wanted whiskey or something, but, no, they all asked for milk!

JAPAN

When we got to the R & R center in Kokura we were issued clean uniforms with our strips sewn on and then allowed to take a long, hot shower and made to look human again. Then we were given a big steak with all the trimmings and ice cream.

I had only been promoted a couple of days before, so I still didn't have orders making me a sergeant. I had to settle for corporal stripes on my uniform, but I proudly wore my Combat Infantry Badge, (CIB). The CIB is a silver rifle on a blue background surrounded by a silver wreath. The CIB is awarded for actual combat against the enemy. It sends a message that you faced the enemy under fire and didn't run. Every soldier wants a CIB, but only about 10 percent ever get one. I still display my CIB with pride.

I hooked up with my friend Jim Ferguson, and we set off for town and a week in a good hotel and shopping, sightseeing, and just having fun. Jim was the radio operator for the regimental commander and worked in the commander's warm command post communications vehicle.

At the hotel was a restaurant, a barber, and a bath that I took advantage of every day. The bath was like a small pool with water hot enough to cook a lobster, or so it seemed. After my bath I would get a shave from a female barber then a massage. It was really wonderful.

Jim and I went sightseeing and shopping with our guide, a girl named Itiko (pronounced it-E-ko). We traveled around town by rickshaw, a two-seat carriage pulled by a little guy on a bicycle. I went to a store that sold china and bought a ninety-six-piece set of china, then had it shipped to Frank's mother in Milledgeville. Frank was my best friend, and his mother always treated me like one of her sons. I didn't say good-bye to her when I left Milledgeville, and this was my way of apologizing to her.

After a week in Kokura, Jim and I headed back to the R & R center for our trip back to Korea.

I took a whole case of milk back to the guys in my platoon.

WINTER

Summers in Korea were hot, humid, and at times downright miserable, but the winters were brutal! In the mountains the temperature would go down to forty degrees below zero. I'm not talking about wind chill factors, I mean Fahrenheit! I've never experienced temperatures that cold, but in January and February it was common to see ten and twenty degrees below zero.

Climbing up the mountain trails was very difficult, especially with heavy equipment on your back. The trails were frozen over with ice and snow and were very slippery. For every two steps up you would slip down one. I solved the problem by wrapping barbed wire around my boots. The barbs were like little spikes that dug into the ice.

My squad went on patrol in January, and there was so much ice and snow that it was easier to walk in a frozen stream than over ground. W stopped for a rest, and I sat on a boulder and leaned back against a frozen waterfall—so much about the myth of running water not freezing.

68

We spent most of the night waiting along a path hoping to capture a prisoner, but we didn't have any luck. Because we had to stay still and quiet for so long, some of us got frostbite. Frostbite is painful and can cause serious medical problems such as losing fingers and toes. A couple of days after the patrol, all my toenails turned black, and the medics removed them to prevent infection. I was miserable for a few days until they started to heal.

Back in reserve I was told that I had my thirty-six points and could go back to the States in a few days. It's strange, but I didn't want to go and leave my platoon and my buddies. They were my family, and I just wanted to stay with my platoon a little longer before going back to the States. I asked the commander for permission to stay longer, and he granted an extension on my tour. Some of the guys thought I was crazy, but they didn't understand that I didn't have a home to go back to and that they were my family. Before the old man (commander) granted my extension I sat down and had a talk with him, and he understood and knew where I was coming from, so he granted my request.

The regiment set up a shower point about a mile from where our squad tents were, and I walked to the shower to get clean uniforms and a very welcomed hot shower. The outside temperature was probably about twenty degrees with about a foot of snow on the ground. The walk to the showers wasn't bad, but coming back was very tough! Before taking a shower we had to take off our old, dirty uniforms, throw them in a pile, and get clean uniforms that had been impregnated with some kind of chemical to prevent disease. The only things we didn't throw into the pile were our parkers, field jackets, hat, and boots.

Well, guess what? When I came out of the shower and put on my clean clothes, some son of a bitch had stolen my boots! We had Korean civilians working in the area, and I'm sure it was one of them.

I put my field jacket around one foot and a couple of towels around the other foot and made my way back to the squad tent. My feet were not fully healed from the toenails being removed, and walking back was very difficult. The supply sergeant laughed like hell when he gave me some new boots, but I sure didn't see any humor in the experience.

I wouldn't be going back on the line with my platoon, and instead it was time to say good-bye to my friends. I would miss them all and especially Lieutenant Dan. I had seen so many good men killed and wounded, and it was going to be very hard to try and not think about that in the years to follow.

A few months before, I had written a poem that I would think about for years to come.

It seems that my sister Betty had contacted the American Red Cross and asked them to find out if I was okay and why I hadn't written since arriving in Korea. The truth is, I didn't think anyone cared.

One day while sitting in my bunker trying to keep warm, a Red Cross guy came in to pay me a visit. I explained why I hadn't written, so he gave me some Red Cross stationary and a pen and sat with me while I wrote a letter to my sister.

While he sat there, he read some stuff that I had written on a piece of cardboard from a C ration box. He asked if he could take it with him and try to have it published in *Stars and Stripes*, the military newspaper. I let him take it, but I don't know if it was ever published. We didn't get the newspaper on the front line. He gave me a tooth brush, tooth paste, and some stationary when he left. All the items had the little Red Cross on them.

This is what was written on the cardboard:

The Punch Bowl

It was late November when the 5th Regimental Combat Team moved onto the MLR (main line of resistance) at the Punch Bowl. There are two mountain ridges running parallel to each other with a sort of valley in between forming a bowl effect. It's about fifty miles north of the 38th parallel in the southeastern part of North Korea. There are bunkers along the ridge connected to each other by trenches that seem to run for miles.

It's cold in late November, but the dreaded Korean winter is yet to come. Sometimes when the wind is right there is a stench of decomposing bodies of the abandoned enemy dead. The Punch Bowl is an awful place to be. There have been many battles here, and there will be more.

We spend hours of sheer boredom each day looking through the portal of our sandbagged bunker at the hill across the valley. It's cold and damp, and the low hanging clouds cast a gray gloom over the hill across the way. It's a cold gray hill, and sometimes we can see the enemy moving about like little ants in the distance.

My platoon (the counterfire platoon) is here to take sound bearings of the North Korean and Chinese artillery and direct artillery fire on them and destroy their weapons if we can.

When we aren't busy trying to locate their guns, we spend long hours of quiet boredom with the silence only broken by an occasional pop of a rifle or thump of a mortar. Sometimes I can hear the quiet whispering of a buddy praying, but most of the time we just look at that cold gray hill.

The Cold Gray Hill

We were on the line to find their guns
Destroy their weapons and make them run.
No matter how many times we tried, they
kept coming and good men died.
We could hear their bugles sound at night
calling their men for another fight.
Then came that terrible sound, incoming
artillery, round after round.
They came running from the Cold Gray Hill
across the valley and up our hill.
The battle raged throughout the night

and didn't stop till morning's light.
All was quiet, not even a sound, then I
saw them on the ground.
As they lay there so very still, I knew my
friends had been killed.
I wanted to think my friends aren't dead,
they're just resting and asleep instead.
I'll never forget that Cold Gray Hill, and
I'll remember my friends as they sleep.

Corporal Earl Russell
Counterfire Platoon
5th Regimental Combat Team
Korea 1952

Now I was going home, and I would think about these
things for the rest of my life.

Me and Jeff at our fox hole

Me at the Punch Bowl

THE LONG WAY HOME

Instead of leaving from the port of Pusan, this time I went to Inchon to board the ship, USNS *General C. C. Ballou*. We didn't find out until the ship was under way that our final destination was New York Harbor.

At the debarkation center I got a new issue of uniforms with stripes sewn on (now I had four stripes instead of the one stripe I came to Korea with) and ribbons and the most prized thing of all, my CIB.

When we set sail for home our first stop was Japan to pick up a few troops, and then we headed to Hawaii to drop off some guys and pick up some more. On the way to Hawaii we ran into a storm that lasted a few days. The sea was so rough that the entire bow of the ship would go under water when it hit a big swell. When we went to the galley for chow, we had to hang onto ropes going from one stairwell to another. I never saw so many seasick guys in my life. They were throwing up all over the place. I never got seasick, but the others throwing up almost got to me.

When the ship docked in Hawaii, they let us go ashore for a few hours. Three thousand troops invaded Honolulu to stretch their legs and have a little look at paradise before continuing the long trip home.

The next leg of the trip was to the Panama Canal. To me this was the most interesting part of the entire voyage. I've read about and seen calm seas in the movies, but we went through the most incredible calm that can be imagined. The sea was as smooth as glass as far as the eyes could see, and it lasted for a couple of days. I saw whales blowing water up through their blowholes, flying fish, sharks, porpoises, and every type of sea life imaginable. Not only was the sea calm, but it was very hot as we neared the canal. Going through the Panama Canal was an experience that I had only read about in school, and the best part of all these sights was that I had all the time I wanted to just look and enjoy. I was a sergeant this time and didn't have any duties to keep me belowdecks.

After passing through the canal from the Pacific to the Atlantic, our next stop was Puerto Rico to drop off a few troops. They didn't allow us to go ashore at this stop, and we continued our long trip after only a few hours.

When we entered New York Harbor we were greeted by a beautiful "lady," the Statue of Liberty. It was a wonderful sight and made me feel very proud to be an American.

The voyage had taken over a month, and I was so glad to get off that ship.

Coming down the gangplank a big red neon sign was flashing in front of us that said "BAR."

After leaving the ship we boarded a troop train that would take me to Fort Jackson, South Carolina, where I was inducted into the army. I would remain at Fort Jackson until my discharge. I had considered reenlisting but I really needed a break from the army to give me time to cleanse my mind of the Korean War.

I had thought myself to be a warrior after ranger school and being assigned to a fighting regiment like the Fifth RCT. I was wrong. A warrior isn't bothered by killing the enemy, but I was profoundly affected and needed some time to heal.

At the processing center the army wanted me to reenlist and go to Fort Benning to join the cadre training students at the counterfire school. When I said no, I was told I could always come back if I changed my mind. I loved the army, but I hated the killing. I needed time.

MACON

I went out of the gate at Fort Jackson and headed for the highway leading to Macon. I was going to hitchhike because I wanted to be alone, and a bus or train didn't appeal to me at the time. While in Korea I had put all my pay in a soldier's deposit account except ten dollars a month to buy such luxuries as toothpaste and personal items such as that. All my regular pay plus combat pay and overseas pay added up to about $4,000 in cash. All of which was in my pocket. It was probably stupid of me to hitchhike with all that money in my pocket, but in those days there weren't too many nut balls around like today.

When I arrived in Macon I went to the Dempsey Hotel, which was probably the best hotel in town at the time. I had the bellboy bring me some sandwiches and a bottle of whisky, and then I took a long, hot bath and crashed for the night.

The next day I bought some clothes and a car and looked up my sister and her husband, Mac.

I was only nineteen years old and didn't have a clue as to what I was going to do with myself. That night I decided to celebrate my entry into the civilian world with a big steak in the best restaurant I could find. It turned out to be the hotel where I was staying. The restaurant was very nice, with dim lights and a lady in a gown playing a piano, and with waiters standing around with little white linen towels on their arms; it was very proper indeed.

When my steak came I was cutting it and somehow my knife slipped, and I flopped the steak out of my plate and onto the floor. I was so embarrassed that I paid my check and left. Probably nobody saw it or even cared, but I had to get out of there.

After paying a visit to my other sister, Lucile, and my brother, Irvin, I decided to go to Milledgeville. I wanted to confront my Uncle Wallace.

On the drive to Milledgeville my mind was spinning. It would be the first time back there since I heard those words, "Get out."

As I drove through town the memories came flooding back. I passed by Frank's house and Junior Gladin's house, but I didn't stop, as much as I wanted to. Instead I drove directly to my uncle's house and parked in front. I went up on the porch and rang the doorbell. When he answered the door and saw me, he had this startled expression on his face. He probably didn't expect to ever see me again.

Uncle Wallace invited me in, but I declined and instead asked if we could sit on the porch and talk. When I asked him why he felt compelled to kick me out over four years ago, he had a shameful look on his face and said, "It was a mistake, and I didn't mean it to be that way." I said, "How was I supposed to take it when you told me to get out? I was only fifteen years old and had no place to go, but I made it in spite of all that." He asked, "What did you do?" So I told him, "I lied about my age and joined the army." He asked if I had gone to Korea, and I said yes. I didn't go into detail and just left it at that. Before I left he said, "If I had known you were actually going to leave I would have given you some money." I didn't comment. Instead, I shook his hand, got in my car, and drove away. His wife didn't come out the whole time we talked on the porch. I was glad.

With that load off my chest I went to Frank's house to say hello to him and his mother. When his mother saw me, she gave me a big hug and thanked me for the china I sent to her from Japan. Frank had a grin from ear to ear and started asking a hundred questions. We had a lot of catching up to do.

When I told Frank that I had only been out of the army for three days and didn't know what I was going to do or where I would live, he told his mother, and she insisted that I stay with them. She had a spare room and said I could stay there. I accepted but only if I could pay rent and pay for my food. So now I had a home, for a while anyway.

I spent a few days getting reacquainted with old friends and meeting new girlfriends, and I started filling out job applications because my money wasn't going to last too much longer.

I finally accepted a multitask job that entailed installing television antennas, stocking groceries, and learning to be a butcher. I didn't like any of this stuff, but at least it was an income until something better came along. I even filled out an application for the Georgia State Patrol.

Shortly before I came back to Georgia, tornadoes did a lot of damage in central Georgia, and that's why part of my job was installing new antennas. In those days everyone had tall antennas on their roofs, and I installed a lot of new ones.

One day I got a call about one of my job applications, so I went to the business for an interview. On my application I had to list all of my army training. The interviewer looked over the form, looked at me and said, "You know, Sergeant, the first time I have a requirement for a ranger, you're the man I'll call!"

I said, "To hell with civilian life!" I went straight to the recruiting office. I had only been out of the army about four months, and the recruiter said I could keep my sergeant stripes.

After thinking about this for a couple of days I decided to talk to the air force, because it was a noncombative service. I didn't want anymore shooting at people and getting shot at. So I gave up one stripe and joined the air force with three stripes and my choice of air force bases and any career field that I qualified for.

Before I went to Atlanta to be sworn in, I talked my friends Frank Garnto and L. K. Sanders into joining with me. They had to go to Lackland Air Force Base for basic training, but that wasn't going to be a problem for them because they had both gone to the same military school (GMC) that Lieutenant Dan and I had gone to. Besides, air force basic is like a Boy Scout camp compared to the army.

I would always regret changing to the air force because I really did love the army. Not only that, but I could have been a senior noncommissioned officer by the time I was twenty-five.

AIR FORCE

I said good-bye to Frank and L. K. and boarded a Greyhound bus to Montgomery, Alabama, where Maxwell Air Force Base is located. I chose Maxwell from several bases offered, but I don't remember the logic of my selection.

When I arrived at the bus station in Montgomery I followed my orders and called wing headquarters at the base. About an hour later I was picked up by a sergeant in a staff car who took me to the personnel office on the base. I turned over my records to the personnel officer, a lieutenant colonel, who promptly disappeared and left me sitting outside his office. After awhile he opened the door and said, "Come with me, airman." He had called me an "airman," and I thought that was really funny. I don't remember if I snickered or not, but when he called me an airman, I felt like I should be flying around or something! This air force thing was going to take some getting used to.

The colonel asked me what career field I would like to enter. I told him that all I knew about the air force was that they flew aircraft, and they had support personnel. He said, "I see by your records that you have extensive experience with weapons. How would you like security police?" I said, "No, sir, that's like permanent guard duty, and I had enough guard duty in the army." "Well," he said, "How about food service?" "No, thank you, sir, I don't want to be a cook." The colonel said, "Tell you what, Russell, take a couple of hours and walk around the base and look around, and if you see anything that appeals to you, come back and tell me. Then we'll see if you qualify for that field."

So off I went to explore the base. I went into hangars and looked at the planes and just wandered around all over the place. I was still in civilian clothes and couldn't believe that nobody challenged me when I was looking over the aircraft. As I walked down the street I saw two airmen working on a telephone line. One guy was up on the pole, and the other guy was tossing rocks at his butt. They seemed to be having fun. I stopped at the cafeteria for a sandwich, and here came the same two guys. Now they were throwing ice at a waitress. These guys were really having fun. I went back to the personnel office and told the colonel, "I want to be a telephone man." So began my air force career as a telephone technician.

I reported to the first sergeant at the communications squadron, where I would stay for about a year. I was learning more about my new service and the difference in the language. A battalion was now a wing, a company was now a squadron, and a platoon was now a flight. It took me awhile to get used to the change. My heart was still army.

The first sergeant assigned me to a barracks and told me

to stay there until he told me what to do. I picked out a bunk, made my bed and did exactly what the first sergeant told me to do. In the army you followed orders exactly, no matter what. After about a week of hanging around the barracks doing nothing, I was lying on my bunk when the first sergeant and executive officer walked into the barracks. They stopped by my bunk, and I snapped to attention for the officer (still in my civilian clothes), and the sergeant said, "What the hell are you doing here?" I said, "I'm doing what you told me to do—stay put until you tell me what to do." He said, "Come to the orderly room." Either the guy had a lot on his mind, or he was two bricks short of a load.

When I went to the orderly room, he gave me a clearance form with all these places I had to go clear in on the base—finance office, personnel office, supply to get my new uniforms, and a bunch of other places. He reassigned me to a room instead of the open bay in the barracks. I went to the first sergeant's office and asked if I could go to Georgia and get my car and clothes. He said, "Sure, see me when you get back." I did see him when I got back, about a week later! He said, "Where the hell have you been?" I said, "You told me I could go to Georgia and get my car, Sarge." He said "Okay." I'm telling you, the guy wasn't all there.

Next I had to go to the range to qualify with the M1 carbine. This was finally something I could relate to since I had lived with a carbine for over a year in Korea. It hadn't been that long ago either.

When I got to the range I was flabbergasted! I thought we would be required to qualify at two hundred yards like in the army, but instead it was a one-thousand-inch range. That's less than thirty yards. I couldn't believe it!

To qualify the perfect score was 200, and I got 200. Later on I discovered that it was the only perfect 200 on the entire base. The range personnel checked over my targets several times to make sure I wasn't using an M1 pencil to punch holes in the targets. What did they expect? I had fired thousands of rounds with my carbine in Korea and even slept with it in my fart sack in very cold weather so it wouldn't be useless when I needed it most.

The score got me a write-up in the base newspaper and a little wooden plaque, but best of all, a three-day pass.

I only fired the carbine two or three times the entire seventeen years I spent in the air force.

After Korea I never shot at a man or even a living creature.

I found out the hard way that the telephone career field was terrible for promotions but red hot for overseas assignments. The career field was classified as critical and almost impossible to get out of to retrain into another field. To get promoted you had to be tested for a higher skill level in your field and only if there was a vacancy on your base for that level. Once you obtained the next level, there had to be a vacancy for the next higher rank. It was a lose-lose situation until the air force changed its promotion policies many years later to be similar to the navy—promotions on test results, performance, decorations, and time in service. The army promoted on skill and performance.

As it turned out, though, had I been in another career field, I wouldn't have spent nearly as much time overseas as I did. I spent nearly fourteen years overseas and had the privilege of either living in or visiting thirty-six countries. You can't buy that!

I soon started my on-the-job training (OJT) as a telephone man working along with my roommate, Thomas Yako. We grew into great friends over the next year and had some very good times together.

My OIC (officer in charge) of the outside plant telephone personnel became a good friend too. His name was Lieutenant Donohue. He was single and used to keep a change of clothes in my room so he could change after work and go out with Yako, me, and our girlfriends. In the army you would never see officers and enlisted personnel hanging out together. He was young, single, and probably didn't have too much in common with the other officers at his living quarters.

One night, rather, early one morning, one of the guys came in my room very drunk and woke me up. His name was Charlie, and he said, "I understand you are a combat veteran transferred over from the army." I said, "Yeah, what about it?" He said, "Let's go out in the parking lot and see how tough you are." I said, "Charlie, it's 2:00 a.m., and I'm not getting out of bed for you or anybody else. I was a soldier, not a street fighter. So go back to your room and drink some more aftershave lotion or whatever has your mind screwed up and leave me alone." He never did bother me again. I guess one of the guys in the orderly room told him

I came from the army. I didn't. He was a good guy until he drank.

Charlie played on the baseball team with Yako and me. He was a very good catcher, and Yako and I played outfield. Yako had an arm like a rifle. My arm wasn't great, but I had a good bat. After every game the team would always have a couple of beers together. The air force was much more social than the army, and that part I liked.

One night Yako and I were barhopping in my car that I kept spotless inside and out. It had been raining for the past three or four days, and none of the "honky-tonk" bars had paved parking lots. The traffic from cars going in and out of the parking lots of one of the bars we went to had made the red mud into soup. My good buddy Yako slipped and fell on his butt going back to the car. I said, "Yako, don't you dare sit on my seat with all the mud on your ass!" He said, "Don't worry; I'll sit on the floor mat." So he took the floor mat, which is all covered with mud from all the getting in and out in the muddy parking lots, and turned it upside down on my seat and sat on the clean side of the mat. I could have killed him! The next day I made him have my car cleaned by a professional.

Another time, Yako and I were in our telephone truck on base when we saw all these emergency vehicles with lights flashing on the street by a water tower. A guy on top was about to commit suicide. Since we couldn't go down the street, Yako drove down the street on the other side of the tower. Buildings were blocking the view for the air police on the other street, but we could all see the guy on the water tower. Yako stopped the truck and started yelling, "Jump,

jump," as loud as he could! I said, "Yako, get back in the truck and let's get the hell out of here." He got back in, and we left in a hurry. We could have been in big trouble for that one. That's my buddy Thomas Yako. It was never dull when we were together.

I got orders for overseas duty in Germany and would be leaving in a couple of weeks with a two-week leave on my way to New York, where I would ship out. I could have had a thirty-day leave, but I didn't have a home to go to so I only took fourteen days.

I stopped by to see my sister Betty and then my brother Irvin and my other sister, Lucile, and said, good-bye again. It seemed as though I was always saying good-bye.

I went to Milledgeville to spend a few days with some friends and to see my Uncle Wallace for the last time.

I had forgiven him for breaking my heart six years earlier when I was fifteen; now I was twenty-one.

I told my uncle that I didn't hold any animosity toward him and had long ago forgiven him for his mistake. When I said, "Good-bye," he had tears in his eyes, and so did I. He was the only father I ever knew. I still haven't been back inside that house where I grew up. It was the last time I would see my uncle alive. He died three years later.

GERMANY

Instead of flying to New York I decided to take a train since I had time to kill before reporting in at my destination.

When I said good-bye to my older sister, Lucile, she said, "Be sure to call and let me know that you got to New York safely; call collect." Well, when I got off the train at Grand Central Station I called my sister collect. She refused to accept the call. I could have paid for the call myself, but I felt so rejected and disappointed that I just didn't bother. I should be used to being rejected by my family by this time, but I wasn't. My other sister, Betty, is the only member of my family who hasn't rejected me.

My orders said to report to Manhattan Beach Air Force Station, where transportation would be provided to my new assignment in Germany. I thought the beach would be nice for a few days, but I was wrong. Manhattan Beach was in Brooklyn, and there was no beach.

I did have a few days to explore New York and get lost on

the subway a couple of times. I didn't like Brooklyn at all, and I wouldn't wish that place on anyone. Coney Island was a short distance from the air force station, and I went there a couple of times and had a lot of fun. It's probably one of the most well-known amusement parks in the world, and I'm glad I had a chance to go there.

Leaving Manhattan Beach Air Force Station, we boarded an airplane for a long flight to Germany. The plane stopped at Lajes Air Base in the Azores to refuel and allow us to stretch our legs and look around a bit.

Our next and final stop was at Rhein-Main Air Base in Frankfurt, Germany.

It was odd, but the first thing I noticed about Germany was the smell. It wasn't unpleasant but different. In the years to come and many countries that I visited, almost every country had a distinctive smell. None would even compare with the aroma of Korea though.

Now it was on to my home to be for the next three years, Landstuhl Air Base.

When I signed in at the 807th Tactical Control Squadron, I met my roommate and future friend, John Ramsey. John and I became very close friends and would do a lot of traveling around Europe together.

It was late in the afternoon, and I couldn't process in until the next day. So I decided to go to a movie. I had some time to kill before the movie started, so I stopped in at the NCO club. I had about enough time for a couple of beers, so I sat down and ordered two beers. The waitress brought me four beers. It was two-for-one night, but I didn't know that. German beer is stronger than the American beer that I was accustomed to, so, needless to say, I never did go to the movie.

The following day I went back to the personnel office, where John Ramsey worked. John asked me what the rifle pin on my chest was. The sergeant major was standing nearby and said, "That's a combat infantry badge, John. He's been in combat with the army. He's a man." I don't recall ever seeing another CIB the whole time I spent in the air force.

My new duty assignment was working on radio antenna towers located on three mountaintops about twenty miles from the air base. It took me awhile to get used to working four hundred and five hundred feet off the ground, but I eventually learned to like it. We worked at our own pace, and nobody ever bothered the antenna crew. Working in the summer in a T-shirt with the wind blowing high above the ground was kind of nice and a great way to keep cool. The winter was another story. Working in a parka and heavy gloves was bad enough, but we couldn't do much to protect our face against the ice-cold wind. Even working with your back to the wind, your lips would still crack and bleed. Sometimes when you came down after working up there for a couple of hours, you looked like you had been in a fight, with frozen blood on your face. The antenna crew worked hard and played hard, and I liked the camaraderie of the crew.

Another job assignment I would get later on was three hundred feet under ground at a site called, "the cave." It was a highly guarded top-secret facility that was built to withstand a nuclear attack. The cave could house, feed, and provide medical care for about one hundred personnel. It was the Air Control Center for the entire continent of Europe. An amphitheater of desks occupied by high-ranking officers looked down on a huge Plexiglas map of Europe, with three levels of controllers behind the glass marking the progress of every moving object in the air. It was very impressive. Had I not had a top-secret crypto security clearance I wouldn't have been allowed inside the cave. My job was to make sure the telecommunications equipment was operational at all times. We worked in shifts of three days, three nights, and three mids, 0800–1600, 1600–2400, and 2400–0800. Then we got three days off. I hated shift work because your eating and sleeping habits were really screwed up. Thankfully, I only had to do this for about six months, and then I went back to antennas.

After being in Germany for about six months, I came to the conclusion that I was letting a golden opportunity slip by. It seemed that I was always with my buddies when off base, and the only places we went were bars and places where almost all English was spoken, and there was no chance to learn about the German people and their culture, so I bought a car.

I had money saved from the sale of my car before I left the States, so I went shopping and found a sweet little 1951 Opel Olympia that was like new inside and out. I hired a German mechanic to examine the car, and when he gave me a thumbs-up, I paid cash for the car and drove away with a big smile on my face. Now I could see Europe the way I wanted, exploring on my own.

I got an international driver's license, international insurance, and green card auto pass and a European road atlas. My buddy John Ramsey got me a stack of orders that listed all countries of Europe except Communist or Socialist countries that I was allowed to visit because of my security clearance. I probably had about fifty sets of orders complete with the commander's signature. John even gave me an ink pad and date stamp. The only thing to do now was do it!

John and I drove to Paris, Amsterdam, and Munich, and to as many places as time and distance would allow. I went to Heidelberg a lot because it was a wonderful place to spend weekends. One summer I even took a fourteen-day leave and drove to Lapland, inside the Arctic Circle in Sweden.

Many times on weekends, officers getting in their flying time would let us know where they would be going and how many seats would be available. It was a great opportunity to go to a lot of places. I kept a book of American Express travelers checks, and I had the orders that John acquired for me, so I was always ready to go.

One of the pilots told me I could fly to Athens with him the next day, and I was ready to go and looked forward to seeing that ancient city for the first time.

The night before the flight a couple of guys and I went to a local gasthaus for a few beers. It was snowing, and when we came outside to get in my car to go back to base, I threw a really hard packed snowball and hit my buddy in the mouth and gave him bloody lips. I felt so bad that I told him he could have my seat on the plane to Athens the next day. The C-47 military transport crashed into Mount Vesuvius, and there were no survivors. I lost my buddy, and all because of a damned snowball. It should have been me.

On one of my trips to Munich I ran into my friend L. K. Sanders. We hooked up and went to the Hofbrauhaus, picked up a couple of girls and had a great time partying in that wonderful old city. It was really good to see my friend from Milledgeville. As it turned out, L. K. was stationed at a small air force station not far from Munich in a town called Freising, a very lucky assignment.

Instead of always going to big cities all over Europe, usually I spent my time in small towns and villages. I would drink beer with the locals in small gasthauses (bars) and get to know the people. I learned enough of the German language so that I was comfortable traveling and ordering food in restaurants. The younger Germans spoke a little English, but the older ones didn't speak any at all. With bits and pieces of German and English mixed with sign language, we managed to communicate. I very rarely encountered any hostility, and when I did, it was usually with a young man who had too much to drink. Most Germans were cordial and easy to like.

On one occasion I did something that I should certainly be ashamed of, and I am. On base we had a snack bar cafeteria combination that was always crowded. I had lunch there several times a week. A waitress that we called "Rocky" was a local girl who had muscles like a man, hairy legs, and unshaven underarms. Rocky was always in a hurry and always sweating. She had a very bad habit of reaching over my plate to clean up empty dishes and to wipe off the table. I asked her to please not do that, but it didn't stop her. One day I had enough and told her, "Rocky, if you do that again, I'll stick you with my fork!" Sure enough she did it again, and, as promised, I stabbed down with my fork, expecting her to jerk her hand out of the way and realize that I was serious about her reaching over my plate. Well, she didn't pull back, and I stuck the fork right into her hand! She was jumping around screaming all over the place with the fork dangling from her hand. They hauled me out of there and took me to my first sergeant, who promptly took me to see my commander, Lieutenant Colonel Clark. He chewed my ass out for a solid fifteen minutes and restricted me to the barracks for two weeks except when on duty.

You can bet Rocky never reached over my plate again. I later tried to apologize to her, but she wasn't having any of that. Every time I went to the snack bar after that I could feel the manager's eyes on me. I felt kind of like a criminal or something.

The guys on the base were talking about that for months.

My roommate, John, and I spent a lot of time together on weekends, but during my three days off of shift work I usually explored alone.

John was a very intelligent guy, just a little shorter than me, with dark brown hair and an ever-present smile. He was quick-witted and always fun to be with. Some of his favorite expressions when we drank beer at the local gasthaus were,

"The drunker I sit here the longer I get," or, "Take me drunk; I'm home as hell." I've used those many times over the years, always thinking of my friend.

On leaving a local gasthaus on a very cold day, John and I were headed down the autobahn in my little Opel doing sixty-five miles an hour on a slight down grade. John said, "Stop at the next rest stop, I want to pee." It had snowed about twelve inches a couple of days before and warmed up a little and then got very cold again. Without slowing down I steered onto the ramp leading to the restrooms. The ruts in the snow from previous cars had frozen solid, and it was more like a bobsled run than a road. I hit the brakes, and the damn car went faster. There was no way I could do anything, so I just hung on and went along with the flying bobsled. As we shot past the restrooms, John screamed, "Oooooh, shit, we're gonna die!" Well we didn't die, but we shot back onto the autobahn still at the same speed and still cruising along with the same cars as before. Wow! What an adrenaline rush that was. Whew! I don't think John needed to pee any more.

Another time when a couple of guys and I went to Amsterdam in January or February when it was very cold, I didn't want to drive, so we took a train.

We found a hotel, went out to eat, and then started barhopping. About two or three in the morning, I wanted to go back to the hotel and get some sleep. While I waited outside for the guys to come out of the bar where we had been for the last couple of hours, I was sitting on an iron railing by a canal with my feet on the middle rail, sitting on the top rail with my hands in my pockets. I had on a leather jacket and fleece-lined boots, and I was warm.

A lady of the night walked up and started talking to me. In response to her question, I must have said something she didn't like because she gave me a shove, and I went backward over the rail and fell through the ice-covered canal. By the time I broke through the inch-thick ice and got to the steps leading up to the street, I was damn near frozen. She was long gone by that time. I got in a taxi and made my way back to the hotel, where I took a hot shower and thawed out. My jacket and boots were ruined.

When the guys came in they asked where I went. When I explained what happened, they got a big laugh out of my ordeal. It wasn't very funny to me!

One night while walking down the street in the little town of Landstuhl I was unconsciously flipping car antennas with my finger, when all of a sudden a German cop grabbed me from behind, yelling all kinds of things in German that I couldn't understand. I don't know what he thought was going on, but he took me to jail and locked me up for a few hours. I wasn't charged with anything, and they let me go. Not fun!

The next day I said, "John, we need to get away from here and go to Copenhagen for a few days." So we both put in requests for a ten-day leave.

We boarded a train in the nearby city of Kaiserslautern, and off we went. The trains in Europe are so efficient that you can literally set your watch by the train's arrival and departure. All the cars had private compartments with two bench-type seats facing each other and a door with a glass window opening into a narrow little hallway—typical of the trains you see in so many movies.

John was leading the way up the hallway looking for an empty compartment when I said, "Whoa, John, come back. I found our compartment." Sitting in the compartment all alone was a gorgeous blonde. We went in, introduced ourselves, and sat down. Her name was Siv, and she was returning home to Sweden after a holiday in Heidelberg.

When we reached the coast, the entire train pulled onto a huge ferry boat for a trip across the North Sea to Denmark.

John and I went up topside to have something to eat at the ship's restaurant, where they had a big smorgasbord. Siv didn't want to come along, so I brought her a big piece of cake when we returned. While we were on the top deck a seagull dropped a load on the back of my new blue suede jacket and left a big white streak down my back. I couldn't get it out, and my jacket was ruined.

I would later spend many happy days in Sweden with Siv and her family. I would fall in love for the first time.

John and I returned to Germany and fell into our regular routine.

Summer came, and one day John asked me, "Can you drive an eighteen-wheel tractor-trailer truck?" I said, "Sure, why?" He said, "The colonel wants two volunteers to take some of our electronic equipment to France and drop it off at two of our sister units." Actually I had never driven a truck that big, but I figured if I could drive trucks for my uncle at the age of fourteen and fly airplanes, I could drive any old truck. So I grabbed John and made a beeline to the motor pool for a crash course in a big diesel with eleven forward gears. I told the sergeant in charge of the motor pool that the colonel wanted us to get checked out, so he let us practice backing that monster up and driving around changing all those gears. We got certified and were all set to go.

Summertime was really nice driving through the vineyards of Germany and France, with the girls riding their bicycles along the road and wine and beer festivals everywhere.

I was behind the wheel driving along in my T-shirt, and all of a sudden it felt like John stuck his cigarette to my side. I backhanded him as hard as I could in his stomach, and he yelled, "What the hell did you do that for?!" I said, "You burned me." He said, "I'm not smoking!" As it turned out a bee had stung me. I spent the next hour apologizing to John.

It was quite a job driving that big truck through those little towns with their cobble stone streets, but we made it to our first stop in Chatereux, France, unloaded the equipment and went to town for some food.

I couldn't read the menu, so John said, "Let me order for us." When the order came, it was snails! I had never eaten snails, and I didn't want to start now, and neither did John. He didn't know what he ordered. We had some wine to think about it, then more wine. The little bistro only had a couple of people there, thank God, because all of a sudden John grabbed two swords that were crossed for decoration on the wall. We started sword fighting in the bistro, and soon we were escorted out by the French police.

We didn't have to worry about going back to the base to find our bunks. The French police provided sleeping quarters for us. They let us go the next morning. We went back to the truck and started the next leg of our trip with giant headaches.

I was glad to get back to Germany, where I could at least order food and stay out of trouble.

Two and a half years after joining the air force, I was promoted to staff sergeant, the same rank I had when I left the army. Staff sergeant in the Air Force is the same as sergeant in the army.

The Fourth of July came, and it was time to celebrate.

My roommates and I got some M80 firecrackers from supply and picked up some beer and started our celebration. My roommates were John, Terranova, and Stevens. The M80 firecracker is much more powerful than a cherry bomb and is used in military training. After drinking beer all afternoon, we started blasting away with the M80s. Terranova was pretty drunk, as we all were, and decided to throw a bomb. He lit the M80, stuck it in his pocket and threw his Zippo lighter. He was standing there with his fingers in his ears when the M80 exploded and blew a hole in his pocket and really hurt his leg. We took him to the clinic for treatment, and that was the last of our celebration.

I went to Sweden as often as I could, and eventually Siv and I became engaged. After much consideration, Siv decided that she didn't want to leave Sweden, and I didn't want to leave my military life and live outside the United States. So we broke off the engagement and went our separate ways.

In Sweden the sun never sets in the summer, so I decided to explore on my own with my little Opel and a car full of gas cans. So I started north to see Lapland. I drove on dirt roads as far as the Arctic Circle, stopping at little villages along the way. I was heart broken from the broken engagement and wanted some time alone.

Driving back south I fell asleep and ran off the road, breaking a rear spring in the car. I decided if I didn't want to kill myself, I had better sleep for a few hours. I woke up to a crunch, crunch sound on the gravel road and peeked out the window and saw a huge moose with antlers about a yard across. I was very still until he went away because I didn't want to piss him off and risk being turned over on the side of the road. If that had happened, there's no telling how long it would have been before someone came along. Up there you hardly ever saw another car.

After I drove away form Borlange, Sweden, and Siv, I continued going north for about three hundred miles along the eastern border of Sweden, passing through half a dozen small towns. My purpose was to see this very beautiful country and cleanse my mind of the dreams I had of Siv and I living our lives together. It didn't work out.

I drove back to Landstuhl with the Opel tilted to one side because of the broken spring. After being back a few days and having the spring fixed, I traded my sweet little Opel for a 1957 Porsche 1600 Super Speedster.

I drove the Porsche for a few months with every intention of shipping it back to the States. The air force threw me a curve and sent me back a couple of weeks ahead of schedule, so I didn't have time to prepare the car for shipment and to deliver it to the port in northern Germany. I didn't like it at all, but I was forced to sell the car.

My friends gave me a big party, and I went to Frankfurt the next day with a hangover for my flight back to the States.

I had plenty of time to reflect on my experiences while being stationed in Germany.

I had lost a friend in an airplane crash and had lost my fiancé and my heart but had gained so many wonderful experiences.

I had been to many countries—France, Belgium, Switzerland, Austria, Spain, Italy, Greece, Denmark, Norway, Sweden, the Netherlands, and several other countries.

When I wasn't traveling during my off-duty time I would coach Little League baseball for the dependent kids on base. One summer we won the European Championship for dependent military kids, and I even got a commendation for that one. I guess the colonel had forgotten *Rocky*.

Because the base didn't have an Aero Club, where I could keep up my flying skills, I joined a glider club, where most of the members were World War II Luftwaffe pilots. I even found time to play golf at Starnberg, Germany, with a beautiful view of the snow-covered Bavarian Alps.

Yes, I can say it was all worthwhile, and I will carry those memories with me for the rest of my life.

We landed at Keflavik, Iceland, to refuel and stretch our legs a bit before continuing our flight to McGuire Air Force Base, New Jersey.

My little Opel Olympia

WASHINGTON, DC

When I arrived at McGuire Air Force base, I was given the choice of accepting my separation from the air force or reenlisting. I had given a lot of thought to going back into the army, but at the last minute I decided to stay with the air force. My heart had always been with the army, but after four years of the soft life in the air force it would have been very tough to retrain and get physically fit for the much tougher regimen of being an effective noncommissioned officer. I was only eighteen as a platoon sergeant in Korea and very physically fit. But at the old age of twenty-four it would take awhile to get back into shape.

So I told the sergeant who was processing me, "I want to reenlist!" After checking on possible duty assignments, he said, "The only place we can station you is at Limestone, Maine." I said, "Limestone, Maine?! Hell that's almost off the map, as far north as the United States goes!" It gets forty below zero in the winter, and I'm not talking about wind chill factors, either. There's nothing there. Maybe there's a girl behind every tree, but I'll bet there are no trees.

I told the sergeant that I would go back to the army before I would let the air force stick it to me and send me to the most isolated base in the United States.

He took my records and went into the personnel officer's office. He probably wanted to shut me up because I was so loud that everybody was looking at us. After a few minutes he and a captain came back to the desk where I was sitting there mad as hell, and the captain said, "Do you want to go to Washington, DC?" I said, "Sure, I'll go." So I was sworn in, and away I went to Andrews Air Force Base, just outside of Washington.

Looking back with my 20/20 hindsight, I should have taken the assignment to Limestone. My chances of being promoted there were much greater than at a base that was considerably more preferred and was loaded with noncommissioned officers. I was probably thinking with my hormones instead of my brains.

It was probably good that I didn't go back to the army because the war in Vietnam would start in about three years. With my ranger training and combat experience, I surely would have been sent there.

Once I got settled in at Andrews I bought a new Corvette. It was powerful and fast but not nearly as smooth as the sports car handling characteristics of my Porsche. I loved that Porsche; it was really sweet. I wish I could have brought it home with me. Too bad!

The duty at Andrews was more demanding than my other assignments. As a telephone technician I was exposed to technology that I hadn't been exposed to before, and I would learn a lot over the next year and a half.

Washington was a good assignment for a single guy my age. There were thousands of young single women working for government offices all over the area. When off duty I went to a lot of parties and met a lot of girls. But it wasn't all parties and having fun. I also spent a lot of time seeing the historic sights of Washington. I took advantage of the opportunity to see our nation's capital and felt very proud to be an American.

In September 1959 I was assigned to be cordon honor guard for visiting Soviet Premier Nikita Khrushchev. I was close enough to reach out and touch both Mr. Khrushchev and President Eisenhower. It was a real honor to be on that assignment.

On Christmas Eve, December 24, 1959, I had a very serious accident. It had snowed a couple of days before, and now it was very cold with light sand on the freeway on and off ramps. They didn't use salt there; instead, they used sand. The snow had evaporated and left the sand there almost like tiny ball bearings. The freeway wasn't divided by a median but by a concrete strip with bumpy ridges. When I accelerated to get on the freeway, the Corvette slid across the two lanes into the oncoming lanes. I was used to my Porsche with the weight in the rear, and I overcorrected and hit an oncoming car head-on. The impact was in the driver's side, just in front of the door. I took the door off with my body, and the door and I ricocheted off the hood of the other car, sending me flying through the air completely across the freeway and down an embankment. I had five skull fractures and a severed temporal artery. They never did find my pants or my shoes, and I would be in the air force hospital for over a month. I had been on my way to deliver Christmas gifts to friends at a Christmas Eve party. The gifts were never recovered either.

When my buddies brought my mail to me at the hospital I learned that my Uncle Wallace had died a couple of weeks before. I'm sorry I couldn't go to his funeral. He was the only father I ever knew.

My buddies also brought me a copy of the *Washington Post* newspaper with my accident on the front page. With the headline "Airman Crashes on Parkway," you would think I was flying a plane instead of driving a car. After I was released from the hospital I bought a new Plymouth, with a little less power and a little less speed.

I had been at Andrews for about eighteen months, and now I had orders for Korea. I wondered what this assignment was going to do to my memories. It was peacetime with the air force, but it would most certainly bring back memories of all the friends that I lost during the war.

KOREA 1960

Four of us in the communications squadron got orders for Korea at the same time. There was Dickenson, Hall, Spraig, and myself. We were to report to Travis Air Force Base and fly to our destination from there. Travis is near San Francisco and is about three thousand miles from DC. Actually, Dickenson was going to the Philippines, and the other two and I were going to Korea.

Dickenson decided to buy a used Buick, take it to the Philippines, fix it up, and sell it for a huge profit. There was a good market for big American cars among the natives there, and he intended to take advantage of it. The car looked good inside and out, but the engine needed to be rebuilt. It burned so much oil that cars behind it couldn't even see the road for the smoke trail it was leaving.

We all decided to go with him and take turns driving to San Francisco. We drove across country taking Route 66, seeing some of the most beautiful parts of America. It was okay as long as you looked ahead or to either side. But looking back to the rear, forget it. All you could see was smoke. We got pulled over by the cops about fifteen or twenty times on our trip. We didn't get any tickets, only advice from the cops, who couldn't figure out what the hell was wrong with our car. Every couple of hundred miles we had to stop and fill our five-gallon can with used motor oil. It could have cost an arm and a leg to use new oil.

We had an overnight stay at Travis, where we took a shower and got rid of our filthy, oil-soaked clothes.

We left Dickenson and boarded a plane bound for Korea. We stopped at Hawaii and again in Japan, then on to Kimpo Air Force Base, Korea. This time the smell wasn't as foul as the first time in Korea, but it was still bad enough. It was kind of like one big garlic breath.

Once we got to Osan Air Force Base and settled in at our communications squadron, I began to see how very different it was going to be this time around. Our barracks were new; we had houseboys to do our laundry and keep the barracks clean, a very big NCO club, and waitresses in the mess (dining) hall. Yep, this was very different. The first time I was here I had very few hot meals. Almost all my meals were C rations. The only eating utensil I had during the war was a spoon that I never washed. I would clean it with dirt, wipe it off with my shirttail and clip it to a belt loop, where it would hang until it was time to eat again.

Outside the base was a little town called "Chico Village." There were bars there and the usual camp followers that always seemed to gravitate toward military installations.

My roommate was a staff sergeant named Lewis. He was an air traffic controller and a great guy. Lewis and I "confiscated" a Coca-Cola cooler for our room—one of those that opened from the top with two sliding doors. We kept beer in the cooler, with a fitted piece of plywood on top of the beer cans, and soft drinks on top of the plywood. That way if the old man (commander) happened to look in, he only saw the soft drinks, milk, etc., and would think nothing of it. We also "confiscated" a 250-pound set of weights and a workout bench for the barracks. Home sweet home.

The telephone crews had a monumental job that was about to start and would last for over six months. We installed a new telephone exchange, all new cables and telephone lines, and all new telephones over the entire base.

The Koreans were such thieves that all the new telephones had to be bolted to the desks. Otherwise they would be stolen as fast as we could install them. Even with security police and dogs, they would still manage to steal anything that wasn't tied or bolted down. Unlike the Koreans, the Japanese never stole anything. The Koreans were terrible.

On Sunday mornings we would go to "sick call" at the NCO club, where we would have breakfast and bloody Marys to fix our aching heads.

During sick call we had a liars club, and contestants could pay a dollar to go onstage and tell their lie. The winner would get a bottle of booze or something, and second and third place would get something too.

One guy said "I saw a saccharin bird on Okinawa that sang so sweet that diabetics had to wear earmuffs." Another guy said, "Back home in Texas we had a steer so big that his horns cast a shadow half way across Texas." A guy in the audience jumped up and yelled, "Judge, this man should be disqualified because this is supposed to be a liars club, and he's telling the truth. I know he's telling the truth because my old man has a trailer that hauls two of them steers." The guy in the audience won the contest.

One night when a couple of guys and I were going to the O.K. Corral in Chico Village, we walked, with our flashlights, on the earthen wall between rice patties. In the middle of the group of rice patties was a well about ten feet deep with about three or four feet of water in the bottom. As we approached the well a voice yelled, "Hey, hey, help me out of here!" We shined our lights into the well, and standing in the water up to his waist was an airman that had been put in there by his pissed-off buddies. He said, "Get me out of here before my legs freeze off." It was summer so there was no danger of his legs freezing. We said, "We're going to the O.K. Corral to get a rope and come back." After a few beers we headed back to the base, and when we got to the well, the guy was gone. I guess his buddies came back and got him out. Maybe he learned not to piss his buddies off.

I took advantage of a golden opportunity to visit Hong Kong while I was at Osan. A special flight was going there, and when I learned about it, I was one of the first to sign up to go. My squadron approved a seven-day leave for me, so I went.

Hong Kong was a very interesting place with a lot more British influence than I had imagined. It was a fun place to take a leave, with hundreds of bars, nightclubs, and restaurants. While I was there I bought a good camera and some clothes, saw all the sights, and spent too much money. Broke and tired, I went back to Osan.

When I got back and assumed normal duty again I got TDY (temporary duty) orders to go to Kunsan Air Force Base on the southwest coast of Korea, on the Yellow Sea. A team of us was sent to erect some antennas.

One day we were putting up a ninety-foot pole that would support a UHF antenna when something happened that I will never, ever see again. The communications officer, a warrant officer named Mr. Wells, was in charge.

We had dug a ten-foot hole with an auger, and Mr. Wells had ordered a crane to lift the pole and direct it over the hole with a cable attached to the top of the pole. We guided the pole over the hole and signaled the crane operator to release the wench and drop the pole in the hole. When he dropped the pole, it went flying into the ground until he finally stopped it with only about three feet sticking up from the hole. If the cable hadn't been attached to the end of the pole, we would have lost it.

I was laughing so hard I was lying on the ground holding my stomach. Mr. Wells was yelling at me and kicking the bottom of my boots, "Get up, Russell. Damn it, it's not funny! Get up, damn it, get up!" I thought the poor guy was going to have a stroke.

We had obviously hit an underground cave, and it was the funniest thing I ever saw.

One night back at Osan in the winter I was at an off-limits bar that I shouldn't have been in. If caught, I would be punished severely by my commander. I don't know why the place was off-limits, but it was, so I knew better than to be there.

It was around midnight, and the air police teamed with the Korean police and raided the place. Everybody was scrambling for a place to hide. One of the girls shoved me into a refrigerator, which was actually a box built into the outside wall of the building. It was about three feet square with a sliding door on the inside of the building; the box itself was uninsulated and was exposed to the cold outside. That's what the Koreans used for cold storage. All the lights were out, and I couldn't see anything, but I soon discovered that somebody else was in there. I reached out and felt a face of a man who could have used a shave. The face whispered, "For God's sake, be quiet, and get your hand off my face!"

When the cops went away and the lights were on again, they opened the refrigerator door and let us out. I discovered that the "face" was my first sergeant. The first sergeant said, "Russell, if you say anything about this, I'll have your ass." It was amazing, but after that night the sergeant and I were pretty good buddies.

While I was in Korea for the second time I took the opportunity to visit Seoul and some of the small towns near the thirty-eighth parallel. During my first time in Korea,

Seoul and the other towns were nothing but burned-out ruins. It had only been about seven years, and the Koreans had done a fantastic job of rebuilding. During the war there were no paved roads in the whole country, but now there were highways and tall buildings and lots of industry. The South Koreans are hard-working, smart people.

I had seen enough and had awakened memories that I had tried so hard to forget. It was time to go back to Osan and move on with my life and stop thinking about the war and my lost friends.

My eighteen month tour of duty was near the end, and I was going back to the States in a few days. I had applied for three bases in California and was given Edwards Air Force Base in the Mojave Desert. It would turn out to be the most interesting assignment of my twenty-year military career.

CALIFORNIA

I left Kimpo Air Force Base on a military aircraft to Tachikawa, Japan. After a couple of hours I boarded a United Airlines Super G Constellation four-engine propeller-driven aircraft bound for San Francisco. It would be the last propeller aircraft I would fly in across the Pacific or Atlantic Oceans except for short military flights to and from some of the South Pacific islands.

On the flight I sat next to a sixteen-year-old girl and her mother who were military dependents. The girl was beautiful and talked to me constantly, but I didn't mind at all. In fact, it was really nice to talk to an American girl after eighteen months of not even seeing one.

We stopped at Wake Island to refuel and have lunch at a navy mess hall and then continued our long flight to the States.

After we landed I said good-bye to the girl and her mother and got a hop to Andrews Air Force Base on an air force

C-118. The hop saved me a lot of money, and it was just as good as flying on a civilian airline.

I had left my car with a friend in Washington and went back to pick up the car and visit for a few days.

After my visit in Washington and at my old squadron at Andrews, I headed for Edwards Air Force Base in the Mojave Desert. It would be a long, lonely drive.

When I started driving across the desert there was nothing there as far as the eye could see, and it was very hot! The road was as straight as an arrow, and it took some effort to stay awake. After what seemed like an eternity I finally reached the main gate at Edwards, got a visitor's pass for my car, and drove about five miles before seeing any buildings at all.

I thought, there is no way I'll ever get used to the desert. It was about 120 degrees, with sand and Joshua trees in all directions. The Joshua tree has twisted branches with dagger-like leaves, and it stores water in its trunk. The trees can grow to eight hundred years. The Mormons named the trees for the prophet Joshua because their outstretched branches reminded then of Joshua raising his arms to God. At first I didn't like the desert at all, but over time I learned to love it. During the day it was very hot, but if you stayed out of the sun, it wasn't bad at all. There was no humidity, and there was almost always a little breeze. At about three o'clock every afternoon the wind would start blowing pretty hard, along with sand that would really damage car windshields and paint.

The wildlife in the desert was pretty amazing to me. Chipmunks that were bigger than the little ones in the East were everywhere, and they stood on their hind legs looking around, kind of like meerkats. There were sidewinder rattlesnakes, road runners, horned toads, kangaroo rats, and even turtles. The desert turtles burrow down under the sand and live on roots for food and water. They live to be two or three hundred years old.

After a very rare rainfall, the desert would come alive with wildflowers. It was very beautiful to see. The flowers would die quickly, though, because of the extreme heat. I only saw it rain a couple of times in the four years that I was at Edwards.

After I got settled in and went to work at the comm. squadron I thought the guys were jerking me around a little, as they often do with new arrivals.

The first work order I got was to install a phone at the monkey house. After doing my other work orders I returned to the shop and turned in my completed work orders except for the monkey house order. The master sergeant in charge of the telephone shop said, "Why didn't you complete this one?" meaning the monkey house. I said, "I thought it was a joke being played on me. Whoever heard of a monkey house on an air force base?" I found out very quickly that there is a monkey house! At Edwards they used chimpanzees instead of humans for testing ejection seats, g-forces on rocket sleds, and other tests. They had other animals for test purposes too.

On one test they used a bear because of his weight, heartbeat, and other reasons. This was to test an escape pod for a B-58 Hustler Bomber. At a very high altitude the pod was ejected, and the bear came to earth safely. The only problem was a very pissed-off bear. He finally had to be tranquilized after several attempts to get him out of the test pod. I don't think the air force used a bear for testing ejection systems after that.

I got to see quite a few flights of the X-15 while at Edwards. After the B-52 mother plane reached altitude and released the X-15 rocket ship, it would then return to the base and buzz the field from a very low altitude of about two or three hundred feet. It was really something to watch that giant B-52 buzz that area with full power. When the X-15 finished the experimental flight, it would land on the dry lake preceded by a loud sonic boom.

Once when I was doing some telephone work at the NASA Administration building, I had the privilege of meeting one of the test pilots, who was also an astronaut. He gave me a scale model of the X-15 that he had set an altitude and speed record with. His name was Joe Walker, and he was later killed flying an F-104 chase plane for an X-B-70 test.

I also installed some telephones in the office of Colonel Chuck Yeager, the first man to break the sound barrier in the Bell X-1 rocket ship.

After that four or five months I was assigned to the communications center at North Edwards, about thirty miles from the main base. I would fill the position that was normally held by a captain. I was in charge of a telephone exchange, telephone operators, inside and outside plant technicians, and cable installers. There was a mix of both military and civil service personnel. It was a big job with a lot of responsibility, but I liked it.

The reason the facility at North Edwards was so far from the main base was the type of testing being done there. All the rocket engines being used for the space program at NASA and all the intercontinental missile engines were tested there.

Edwards was a fascinating place if you like aviation as much as I do. I even had the experience of watching the U-2 spy plane take off and land at one of the isolated airfields at Edwards. Many U-2 flights were made during the Cuban Missile Crisis, and they all were made from Edwards.

After a few months I was relieved from my duty at North Edwards when a captain was assigned to that facility to take over the job that I had been doing until that time.

When I went back to the main base we started installing hundreds of telephones in a very large hangar being converted into offices for engineers working on the X-B-70 Experimental Airplane. North America Aviation was the contractor doing the project, but just after the maiden flight of this supersonic giant, Congress canceled the project. The design research was given to the French and English, who used it to build the Concorde supersonic airplane.

I was lucky enough to be standing near the runway and witness the first landing of the X-B-70. What a sight!

Because of my security clearance I saw a lot of top-secret

projects. One of the projects was the YA-71 spy plane, later to be designated SR-71 Blackbird. It could fly higher and faster than any airplane ever built and still holds that distinction.

On weekends some of my friends and I would go to Ensenada, Mexico, on the Baja California peninsula. It wasn't too far away, and there were great beaches and lots of nightclubs and restaurants. Oh, yes! There were a lot of pretty girls too! I almost forgot to mention that!

Back at Edwards I became a Mason. I was initiated at the Henry H. Arnold Lodge #791 in Rosemond, California, near the base. A few years later I would rise to the level of master Mason at a lodge in Wiesbaden, Germany—a German lodge and a great experience.

A couple of months after President Kennedy was assassinated, I got TDY orders to the White House Communications staff. My job was to precede presidential flights in the continental United States along with a Secret Service agent and arrange for a secure telephone line to be on the tarmac exactly where Air Force One would stop. Then I would open a little door under the plane and connect the telephone line. This had to be done a second or two after the wheels of the airplane stopped.

During the Cold War with the Soviet Union, the White House had a hot line directly to the Kremlin in Russia. The line followed the president everywhere he went. This president was Lyndon B. Johnson. I guess I was selected for the assignment because I was a telephone technician, and I had a top-secret crypto security clearance. That's a security clearance even higher than US senators have. It was good at times, but sometimes it got me some rotten assignments.

After my temporary duty was over I got a job at the noncommissioned officers' club (NCO) to make some extra money and not sit on bar stools so much when I was off duty. I started as a "bar back," or bartender assistant, and by the time I left Edwards I was a full-fledged and skilled bartender. I made more money doing that than I was getting from my military pay.

After almost four years at Edwards I got orders for Wheelus Air Force Base in Libya. It was sandwiched between the Mediterranean Sea and the Sahara Desert. The Libyan Desert is the hottest part of the Sahara, with temperatures reaching in excess of 130 degrees with no humidity.

I had been at Edwards longer than any other place since making the military my career.

LIBYA

My flight originated at Charleston Air Force Base, South Carolina, with a brief stop in the Azores for fuel and a meal and then on to North Africa.

We landed at Wheelus Air Force Base, Tripoli, Libya, on Christmas Eve. I was hoping to arrive on the base in time to go to the finance office and get paid, but it was too late in the day, and everything was closed. So I went to my new squadron and signed in and left a copy of my orders with the CQ (change of quarters), then I went to the NCO club.

When I entered the club I was really surprised at how big and plush it was. It was more like a casino than any air force club I had been in, with slot machines lining the walls of a very long hallway.

I was broke, with only three or four dollars to last for the next three days. I couldn't eat and drink on that little amount of money, so I said, "What the hell," and put a quarter in a slot machine. Would you believe it! I hit twenty-five dollars with my first quarter and headed for the bar.

The club had a huge ballroom and dining room, a circular main bar that would seat about a hundred people, a stag bar, and pool tables, more slot machines, and a couple more bars in other areas of the club.

I ordered a drink, and soon I was talking with a couple of guys sitting next to me. One guy was called Fluffy and the other guy was called Mad Dog—nicknames, of course. When they discovered that I had only arrived a couple of hours ago, my money was no longer any good at the club.

It turned out that Fluffy was a bartender there, and Mad Dog was the head bartender. Mad Dog asked me about the club at Edwards, and I said, "It was a nice club, but not anything to compare with this one. I spent a lot of time there because I was a bartender." His face lit up, and he said, "Do you want a job?" I said, "After I get settled in and find out what my duty is going to be, maybe I'll talk with you about that."

I had just arrived at my new base, hit a jackpot on the slots, got a job offer at the club, and all my drinks were on the house! I think I'm going to like this place.

When I finished clearing in on base I was taken to my duty section, the outside plant telephone shop, and met all the men that I would be working with for the next two years. It was a small shop with only about seven personnel. It was located in a big building with a lot of unused space.

I was given a crew of two men and went out on my first work order. In order to learn procedure at my new base, I wanted to go up the pole at the site of the telephone installation and call in to the test board operator, have the number activated, and connect the wire to the terminal. So I put on my climbing equipment, hooks and belt, and started up the pole. My crew of two was a one-striper and a two-striper, and these guys were laughing like crazy. I couldn't figure why it was so funny to them because I had plenty of experience climbing.

It was hot, and I had taken off my shirt and was working in my T-shirt. When I got to the top where the terminal was located, I put my safety belt around the pole and settled back. The two idiots down below were laughing their asses off, and I soon found out why. When I slid the terminal cover up, all of a sudden about a half dozen six- or eight-inch lizards came flying out of the terminal right onto my chest. I yelled, "Good Lord, I'm going to get bit to death!" I couldn't get away from them because of my safety belt around the pole. It happened so fast, and I was so close, I couldn't tell if they were snakes or what. Their sharp little toenails were sticking my chest through my T-shirt, and I thought I was being bitten. It scared the crap out of me, and I wanted to kill the two guys. It seemed that every terminal was a home for some kind of creature, and after that experience; I learned to step to one side and slide the cover up. It was a prank that was played on all new telephone installers. I nearly had a heart attack, but it really was funny.

After a couple of weeks I accepted the bartender job that Mad

Dog had offered when I first arrived at Wheelus. Actually, Mad Dog's name was Maddox, and he was nicknamed after some famous baseball player, "Mad Dog" Maddox.

He was a big, good-looking guy with black, curly hair and a southern drawl. He came from south Georgia.

When tending bar I met a lot of people and had fun too. I met a guy who would become my best friend in Libya, Ken James. Ken was a very good-looking man who could easily have been a model or a leading man in Hollywood—six feet tall, black hair, and a thin mustache. Sometimes he was a little crazy, too, but always fun to be around.

I remember one night the club was full, and every seat at the main bar was occupied. Ken and I were sitting at a little two-person table near the bar, and he said, "I feel like fighting." I said, "Knock yourself out, Ken." So he got up and elbowed himself between a couple of guys at the bar and took a big sip from one guy's drink. When the guy said, "What the hell do think you're doing?" Ken spewed the mouthful of the guy's drink right in his face. The guy hit Ken in the mouth and knocked him onto his ass. Ken got up and sat back down at our table with bleeding lips, and I said, "Feel better now?" He just grinned.

Another time a good-looking blonde schoolteacher came into the club in the afternoons after school a lot. I said, "Ken, I'm going to take her out." He said, "Not before me you're not." So one day I went to the club, and the beautiful little schoolteacher was sitting there all by herself. I sat down next to her, and after awhile she and I were about to leave together, and in walks Ken. He walked up behind me, spun me around on the stool, kissed me right on my lips, and said, "Been waiting long, Russ?" The girl got up and left the club and wouldn't have anything to do with either of us after that. She probably thought we were gay. I could have killed Ken. He thought it was hilarious. He said, "I told you, not before me!"

One night he said, "Let's go to Tripoli in my new car." He recently had a Ford Fairlane shipped from the States and wanted me to go to a nightclub in Tripoli with him.

Construction was under way on the road to the club with a three-foot-wide ditch across the path. He said, "I'm not going five miles out of my way because of that ditch. I'm going to jump it with the car." I said, "You can't make it, Ken, don't do it!" Well he backed up the street, put the gears in forward and floored it! I screamed, "Oh, hell, Ken, you're going to wreck your car!" I braced myself, and he hit the ditch. The front wheels didn't make it across as he thought they would and instead went into the ditch and stopped the car instantly. If I hadn't braced myself, I would have gone through the windshield. His car was ruined because the wheels and front-end suspension had moved back two or three feet from where they were supposed to be. His car was totaled.

Not long after that I bought a 1954 Chevy from a couple who were returning to the States. The car was like new because the wife took care of the inside of the car, and the husband took care of the outside and mechanical needs.

I drove the Chevy all along the coast of the Mediterranean Sea from Tunis, Tunisia, to Alexandria, Egypt. It was a good car, and I always kept ten gallons of gas in the trunk, five gallons of water with water hoses for the cooling system, and a tool box.

I had always been somewhat of a free spirit, and the cars I owned on my overseas assignments allowed me to do and see things that few people would have the privilege of experiencing.

While at Wheelus I joined the diving club and got my first scuba certification. The base was actually on the coast, with private beaches, an NCO club annex, and the dive club.

Since we were on the coast, I decided it would be nice to have a sailboat. I had never sailed before, so I went to the library and checked out some books on sailing and boatbuilding.

The building my shop was in had some extra space, so I laid the keel and started building a twenty-one-foot sloop. The air force was kind enough to provide me with all the materiel I needed (through my buddies in supply), and I worked on the boat when I found time. The commander came in one day on his weekly walk-through inspection and asked me, "What are you building, Sergeant Russell?" I said, "Colonel, this is an air force base, so I'm building an airplane." Every week he would stop by and ask, "How's that plane coming along?" I said, "Sir, it's coming along just fine, and when it's finished, I'll take you for a ride." He smiled and said, "I look forward to that."

One of my buddies at the parachute shop made the sails for me from the drawings that I gave him.

It took about six months to build, and when it was finished, I got about ten guys and loaded it on a truck and took it down to the beach. Nobody wanted to come along with me on the maiden tryout since I had never sailed before, so I went alone. The boat really moved through the water, and I kept busy with the mainsail and the jib.

The wind was blowing so hard that I was afraid to come about for fear of capsizing, and I was so far out that the coast of Africa was about to disappear. I finally got enough guts to come about, and after tacking about ten miles back to the beach using the beacon on the base water tower as a guide, I finally beached the boast. It was way after dark when I got back. That was the first time I had sailed solo—or with anyone else.

I used the boat often and even kept my promise and took the colonel out one day. When my tour of duty was over a few months later, I gave the boat to the guys in the telephone shop.

Ken and I rented an apartment in Tripoli on the seventh floor looking out at a busy market street. It was the tallest building on the street, and nobody could look into our windows from other buildings. Ken worked at night on aircraft, and I worked outside most of the time in the heat. One day after working in the desert installing a cable to the ammunition storage area about five miles from the base, I was hot and tired, and all I wanted to do was take a cold shower.

The apartment had very high ceilings with large windows—no screens—and shutters that when opened let a breeze blow through from other windows overlooking rooftops from the kitchen area.

When I came into the apartment a note on the refrigerator read, "Russ, please feed Fred." Ken obviously was drinking when he wrote the note because he spelled Fred, "Frex." Fred turned out to be a little kitten.

I opened the shutters, and after my cold shower I sprawled across the bed naked and let the breeze blow across my still-wet body. All of a sudden Fred jumped on the bed and stuck his sharp little claws into my bare bottom. Without thinking I reached back, grabbed him, and tossed him. He went sailing out the window but managed to catch the curtain with his sharp little claws and swung out over the street below and then back inside. He went running through the apartment onto the rear window sill and jumped onto the rooftops. He was gone forever.

Later when Ken asked me where Fred was, I said, "Who is Fred? I saw the note, but I don't know who Fred is."

After a few weeks I finally told him what happened. It pissed him off a little.

I had been dating an English girl for the past few months. Her name was Eunice, and she worked for the British Embassy in Tripoli. She was very pretty, tall, with big brown eyes, brown hair, and a great smile. Eunice was bright and fun to be with. We were almost always together when I wasn't working.

One evening after going out to dinner I drove her to the

compound where she lived with other women who worked for the embassy.

I stopped near the gate, got out, and walked to her side of the car, and, being a gentleman, took her hand and walked with her toward the gate.

Out of nowhere a Libyan policeman with pistol drawn made us get back into my car. The Libyan got into the backseat and, holding the pistol to the back of my head, directed me to a big jail. I think it was actually a prison.

Once we entered the prison they took Eunice in one direction and me in the other. They threw me in a cell about eight feet long and five feet wide with no windows and no lights. The cell had bare floors and smelled of urine. I was more worried about Eunice than about myself and imagined all kinds of horrible things happening to her.

After two days of not seeing either me or Eunice, our friends knew something was wrong. Ken and some of my other buddies went to the air force provost marshal to ask that the air force look for me. They wouldn't, so our friends went to the British Embassy and explained that Eunice and I were always together and something was very wrong.

They conducted a search of all the hospitals and jails and finally found us.

We had been in that hellhole for three days with no food or water. We would have died if not for the British.

We were helped outside and put into an ambulance, where

Eunice went to the embassy hospital, and I went to the air force hospital at Wheelus. I remained there for a couple of days and was treated for dehydration and got some nourishment through IVs.

It seems that we had offended Allah by holding hands in public. I wasn't showing affection, I was only trying to be a gentleman. I've hated the Arabs ever since.

I didn't see Eunice but a couple of times after that because she wouldn't go out and eventually went back to England. The experience was a trauma that was difficult for her to manage. I know she didn't blame me for what happened, but I felt guilty for not being able to protect her.

I belonged to the base Aero Club and took great pleasure in buzzing the camel herders from so low that my wheels almost touched the camels. The Arabs would spend months in the desert rounding up stray animals to take to market in Tripoli.

When I buzzed them they would run for miles, and it would take a lot of effort to round them up again. I learned some obscenities in Arabic and would shout the nasty words at them every chance I got. I should be ashamed, but I'm not. While tending bar at the club I met Beth and her husband, who had just recently arrived in Libya. Beth was small and pretty, a Cajun from Louisiana about five feet three, a 105 pounds, black hair, and brown eyes. She had a little girl about three and a half.

Shortly after arriving at Wheelus they separated, and Beth

came to the club a lot and always managed to sit near my workstation at the bar.

She told me that she was getting a divorce, and she had to leave Libya and return to the States. After her divorce she wrote to me and asked me to come and visit her in Louisiana when I got back to the world.

Mad Dog had gone back to the States, and I suddenly found myself being elevated to head bartender, with twenty-two bartenders on the payroll. With the club being so big we needed that many to rotate shifts to keep all the bars going.

I also took on a couple of more part-time jobs because I wanted to save enough money to pay cash for a new car when I got back to the States.

I got a job with Esso installing communications cable for the oil well pumping stations out in the desert. I got someone to fill in for me on weekends at the club, and the oil company would fly me out to the oil fields on Friday evenings and back to Tripoli early Monday mornings in time for me to be at work in my air force job. I worked about thirty hours each weekend and got paid very well, under the table with no tax. They paid me in Libyan pounds, so I had to have the money converted. I didn't have a work permit, and if the Libyans had found out what I was doing, I would have been in big trouble. I made a lot of money.

Another way I made money was by selling furniture on the black market. I could have gotten in big trouble doing this too!

Most of the military families going back to the States wanted to sell their furniture so they wouldn't have to ship it home. They would take the proceeds and buy new stuff when they got home.

From some of my Arab contacts I would find a buyer, compile a list with photos, and arrange a meeting between the seller and the buyer. The meeting was always at a safe location in Tripoli. I would get a fat commission from each sale.

When my two years were completed I got orders for Eglin Air Force Base in Florida. I hadn't been to Eglin since my ranger survival training at "Camp Rudder" on the Eglin Reservation.

While in North Africa I took advantage of the opportunity to see as much of that part of the world as possible. I visited Malta, Crete, Morocco, Algeria, Tunisia, and Lebanon. Roman Ruins all along the cost of the Mediterranean Sea gave testament to the power of the Roman Empire. I drove my Chevy to some of these places and took military hops to others.

I worked hard while at Wheelus and managed to save about $15,000, which was a healthy sum in the sixties.

When I left Libya I would carry in my memories the terrible ordeal that Eunice went through. She will always have a special place in my heart.

After I arrived in the States I took a commercial flight to Pensacola, Florida, where I bought a new Ford convertible.

I bummed around the beaches and bars and explored the area for a couple of weeks and then went to Eglin Air Force Base and signed in.

My 54 Chevy (Sahara Desert)

FLORIDA

Eglin Air Force Base is the largest air base in the free world with 724 square miles of land and 101,000 square miles of air space. I didn't know that until I was stationed there in the air force. When I was at Camp Rudder, the ranger camp at Eglin, and jumped with a team for a three-day survival exercise I didn't think about those things, or care either, but now I'm here with the air force and new adventures.

Once I settled in at my new squadron I took a weekend trip to Louisiana to visit Beth. I should never have done that because I brought her back to Eglin with me and made the colossal mistake of my life. I married her.

I bought a two-bedroom manufactured home and set it up on base at a location designated for that type of home. The lot was on the edge of a bay, and I could fish from my yard. Each lot was separated by a couple of hundred feet and was private and really pretty nice. Certainly not a typical trailer park.

After a few weeks I got a motorcycle so that each of us could get around without having to schedule the use of my car.
I kept snorkel equipment in my saddlebags and frequently went to Destin, where I would put on my gear and snorkel for crabs. I kept the freezer with a supply of crabmeat, and we had crab salads and other goodies made from my catch.

At the fishing wharf at Destin old men would sit on the piers and watch the crabs inching their way toward the baited traps. When they had caught enough, the traps would be pulled up, and the old guys would go home with their bounty.

A jetty two or three hundred feet from the wharf protected the fishing boats from the sea. The jetty had a path on top, and I could ride my motorcycle out on it and across from where the old men were fishing for crabs. To get to the road leading to the jetty you would have to go about a mile from the wharfs and then about a half mile down the jetty to be across from the crab guys.

I would go out there, put on my gear, snorkel out near the crab traps, dive down, and scoop up the crabs and swim back to my motorcycle while the old men were screaming obscenities at me, I would get about a dozen crabs each time, get on my bike, and get the hell out of there. I was a bad boy!

The workload at Eglin was probably the hardest of any base I had been assigned to. I have heard civilians say many times that the military didn't work nearly as hard as they did. Well that's a bunch of crap! At Eglin we worked fourteen hours a day, six days a week at very low pay and no compensation for overtime. The entire base at Eglin was being reorganized, and we were kept busy day and night installing and moving telephone equipment.

In 1966 the army was actively seeking qualified non-commissioned officers. They needed helicopter pilots and other specialized positions because of the escalated war in Vietnam.

I applied for the program and qualified as a communications officer. I really wanted helicopters, but my color vision let me down. As a civilian pilot I could read aviation colors, but I couldn't pass the military color test.

All I had to do was report to Fort Rucker, Alabama, and be sworn in as an army warrant officer. I would be discharged from the air force during the same ceremony. At the last minute I withdrew my application for the army warrant officer program and remained in the air force. I'm glad of that decision now because if I had gone back to the army, I would never have fathered the two wonderful sons that I have now.

It wasn't long before I got orders for Johnson Island in the South Pacific. It was a one-year tour of duty and extremely isolated with all male personnel. No women were allowed on the island, period!

Because it was a top-secret assignment and men only, I had to be interviewed by an air force psychiatrist. The doctor was a major, and after a few minutes he asked me, "Have you ever had any sexual desires for your mother?" That really pissed me off, and I said, "That would be kind of hard to do, doctor, because my mother died when I was two years old, but I'll consider your mother." I thought the poor son of a bitch was going to faint. He yelled at me, "Get out of my office!" I passed the exam with flying colors, and I was on my way to the South Pacific. I had the trailer moved to Louisiana so Beth and the girls could be near her family. I spent a couple of weeks with them and departed for San Francisco, where I would board a plane for Hawaii.

JOHNSON ISLAND

The first stop after leaving San Francisco was Hickam Air Force Base, near Honolulu, where my home squadron had its headquarters.

After signing in I was scheduled to go on a flight to Johnson Atoll the following morning. All passenger flights to Johnson Atoll were provided by Air America, which is actually run by the CIA (Central Intelligence Agency).

The plane was a C-124, a very large cargo type aircraft. Since there were no women allowed on the island, we had a steward instead of a stewardess. Johnson Atoll is located about 850 miles southwest of Hawaii, and with only about two hundred miles to go before reaching the island, we lost an engine. When the engine stopped, it sure got my attention. All I could see below was the Pacific Ocean, and all I thought about was all those hungry sharks swimming around waiting for me. We continued the flight on three engines.

It wasn't long before the pilot announced, "Look on the port side and you'll see your new home." I looked but I didn't see anything. Finally I spotted a little speck in the vast ocean below and said, "You mean to say this monster of a plane is going to land on that?!" The island was so small that it had to be extended by dredged coral from the sea to make it long enough for a runway.

No vegetation was on the island, and it was only eight feet above sea level. The atoll was surrounded by a coral reef that was about a mile out from land, giving it a doughnut shape. Between the island and the reef was a beautiful lagoon.

Approaching the runway we were so low that the wheels were barely above water. When we touched down and taxied to a stop at a security building (actually a Quonset hut), two guys were holding up a panel stretched between two poles that read, "Hello Ass Hole!" For every incoming plane, the panel went up to great new arrivals. The island commander let the guys have their fun.

After getting off the plane everyone was searched for photographic equipment. Then we were photographed and given a security badge with our photo, which had to be visibly displayed on our person at all times. About a hundred military personnel were on the island and a handful of civilian people. The civilians were all employed by the Atomic Energy Commission.

The mission of the island was to hold an atomic bomb test every year. We would build up to the test and count down to detonation. There was no actual explosion of the bomb, but the test was conducted as if it was. Then it would take about thirty days to break down what took about ninety days to prepare. Then debrief and carry on normal activity, which wasn't very much. The island also had intercontinental ballistic missiles and some top-secret stuff that even after forty years I still won't mention.

It was customary to take a newcomer to the club and welcome him with a beer and then on to be introduced to the old man. My new commander was a lieutenant colonel and a great guy, a man of medium build and gray hair around the ears and a very warm smile.

The club was a large covered patio with two palm trees protruding through the roof and a bar at one end of the patio with a little office behind the bar.

I was sitting at a table having a beer and talking with the guys that had greeted me when all of a sudden a beer can came flying through the air from a table with a couple of sailors in T-shirts wearing their little white hats. We just looked at each other and said nothing. In a few minutes a full can of beer came flying from the table of swabbies and splashed beer on my clean, pressed uniform. This time I went over to the table and said to the sailors, "If you guys are looking for trouble, you just found it." One of the sailors said, "No, Sarge, we aren't looking for trouble!" So I turned and started walking away. Then I heard, "Hey, Sarge!" I turned around and caught a fist right in my mouth. I stumbled backward but didn't fall. The sailor started walking toward me when I kicked him so hard between the legs that I lifted him off the floor. I jumped on top of him in a rage and with my fingers behind his ears and thumbs in his eyes, started pounding his head on the concrete floor and rubbing his head from side to side on the rough floor. The guys had to pull me off before I did permanent damage to the idiot, or worse.

When I stood in front of the colonel with my missing tooth and blood on my uniform he asked, "What happened to you?" I said, "You won't believe this, sir, but I fell down the steps getting off the plane." He didn't say so, but I'm sure he knew better than that. He sent me over to see the island doctor.

When the plane had finished off-loading and refueling, reloaded, and engine fixed, I got on board and flew back to Hawaii to get my tooth fixed. Sitting across from me was the stupid sailor going back to get his head fixed at the navy hospital in Honolulu. I had taken all the hair off the back of his head down to the bone. He had a permanent bald spot about the size of an orange. I wasn't sorry at all. You can bet he never came near me again when he returned to Johnson Island. I had a pin and crown put in where my old tooth used to be.

When I got back to the island the guys from my telephone shop said, "Lets go over to supply and get you a horse." I said, "Horse? What the hell are you talking about?" It turned out that everyone on the island could get a bicycle and paint it any color they wanted. The bikes were known as horses. I painted my horse international orange— bright fluorescent orange you could see a mile away. One of a kind on the island! I loved my horse!

We only had three guys in my telephone shop; that was too many for the workload. Boredom was a serious problem on the island, and during the year that I was there we had several suicides. I intended to keep busy so the time would pass quickly.

My lips and swollen mouth had healed, and sitting at the bar one day after work I struck up a conversation with the bar manager. He was a big black senior master sergeant and a very nice guy. I told him that if he wanted to hire the best bartender on the island, I was available. He said, "Proud of yourself, aren't you!" I said, "It's true, Sarge. I was head bartender at one of the biggest clubs in the air force with twenty-two bartenders on the payroll. I'm fast and can mix anything, and my inventory and cash is never short." He let me get behind the bar for about an hour to show him my skills, and he hired me.

With all the off-duty jobs I had as a bartender, you would think I was a heavy drinker. The truth is, I wasn't, and I never drank while working the bar. The part-time jobs I had as a bartender actually earned me more money than I was paid by the air force.

Now I had my air force job and a bartender's job, and I had joined the dive club. It was called "The Pacific Atoll Divers." Later on I would get my scuba instructor's certification and teach classes in my spare time. Over the years I probably instructed and certified a thousand divers.

Johnson Atoll had beautiful coral formations with unbelievable sea life—ten-foot-long moray eels that weighed a hundred pounds, giant manta rays with sixteen-foot wingspans, all kinds of sharks, including white tips, blue sharks, hammer heads, and several other species. It was a paradise for scuba divers and snorkelers, and I went diving almost every day in the crystal-clear water.

After only about two months Beth stopped writing, although I was writing two or three times a week I knew I had a problem. My marriage was in trouble, but I was hoping that we could work things out and make it last. I tried not to think about it and stayed busy taking on even more jobs. I worked at the lapidary hobby shop and learned all about cutting and polishing stones. I worked at the movie theater as an assistant manager. When I had any free time, I went diving.

At Johnson Island we had a "class six" ration book with stamps to buy our allotted monthly booze. Class six was the military designation for bottle shop. For some reason the book had stamps for seven bottles of whiskey a week, far too much for even the hardest alcoholic.

During our monthly commander's call, a mandatory information meeting held by the commanding officer, the colonel made an announcement. He said, "Gentlemen, our class six rations have been cut from seven fifths a week down to five fifths a week." I stood up and said, "Sir, what the heck are we going to do on weekends?" The colonel said, "Shut up and sit down, Russell!" I got a big round of applause for my question, and even the colonel smiled.

The island had a twenty-five-foot fishing boat and took fishing parties out beyond the reef for deep sea fishing. One day it went out with six fishermen, some of whom were Hawaiian contractors working on the island. The weather had been bad for a few days with high winds and rain causing very big waves breaking over the reef. There was a pass to get in and out of the lagoon, and with those big waves the timing had to be right, otherwise you were in trouble. The operator of the boat missed his timing, and the boat was tossed upside down, killing everybody on board.

Two of my buddies and I were loading our fourteen-foot-long raft with diving equipment to go diving out near the reef. We heard the distress call coming from someone over the radio asking the navy to respond. We opened up the throttle on our raft's engine and was at the scene long before the navy divers arrived.

Butch Ribet, Joe Richard, and myself had recovered the bodies by the time the navy ship got there. The noise of the crashing boat and the blood in the water had attracted sharks to the area, and we wanted to get the job done as quickly as possible. It was a very sad day on the island.

The Hawaiians on the island had a little club of their own and would cook the fish they caught and have a luau for the Hawaiians and invited guests. I tried but could not get in their club.

After the recovery of their Hawaiian friends, they looked at me in a different way and invited me to their club. One of the men was a tall (about six six) muscular guy of royal Hawaiian heritage by the name of George Kalamalamala. Big George assumed the role of my protector and made my life easier, not only on Johnson Island but also in Hawaii.

I had gained a lot of respect on the island and could do almost anything I wanted to do.

Not long after the boating accident the dive club held its annual election, and I was elected president of the Pacific Atoll Divers. Now I was probably the busiest guy on the island. I didn't mind, though, because it made the time go by faster, and I had little time to think about Beth and what I assumed to be her infidelity.

A big ship was scheduled to arrive at the island in a few days, and the island commander was worried about the possibility of the ship hitting the under seas communications cable in the shipping channel. There was no chart of the cable's exact location, and if the ship broke the cable, it would be disastrous.

I went to the colonel and told him that with his help the divers could chart the cable for him. All we needed was about a hundred Clorox bottles from the island laundry and several reels of parachute cords. The Clorox bottles were big five-gallon containers and being white would really show up in the sun. The divers would tie the lines attached to the cable. It would take us a couple of days to complete the mile of Clorox bottles. All the colonel had to do was get the Department of Defense and Atomic Energy Commission to approve an aerial photograph. The aerial photo turned out great with the Clorox bottles so white and bright in the sun. They looked like little white dots showing the way through the channel.

If it's one thing I'll miss from Johnson Atoll it's the food. Our dining facility, or mess hall, was staffed with chefs and cooks hired by the Atomic Energy Commission. They were highly paid and very good. We were often served prime rib, steaks, shrimp, omelets, chocolate éclairs, all kinds of salads, and just about anything we wanted. Although I worked constantly and went diving when I wasn't working, I still managed to gain weight. I ate too much and drank too much scotch.

Sometimes to break the monotony some of the guys (after drinking a little too much) would play chicken with their "horses." One street ran the length of the island, end to end. It was the only street on the island and had a white stripe down the middle. A guy and his horse would start at each end and go as fast as possible down the center line and see who would chicken out first. Everyone would bet on his favorite horse. Sometimes they wouldn't chicken out and crash head-on into each other. They just didn't give a damn. Sometimes the horse riders would get bruised and cut up pretty good. The game was forbidden on the island, but they did it anyway. I'll miss the fun.

It was time for me to go, and my friends told me to look down at the club as the "Freedom Bird" climbed out over the island. As I looked down I saw a bright orange banner that said, "Good Bye Ass Hole."

On the Air America plane with me going back to Hawaii was my friend Big George. I spent a few days with him near Honolulu before going to see Beth and the girls. I was hurt and angry.

WIESBADEN, GERMANY

I enjoyed the few days in Hawaii with my friend Big George, but now it was time to face Beth and find out why she had stopped writing.

It was a long trip to Louisiana, and when I got there, I was in for a shock. The manufactured home that I had moved from Florida was now gone. She said it was destroyed by floodwaters along with everything in it. Now she lived in an expensive up-scale apartment. I had been sending her money every month but not nearly enough to support her new lifestyle. She still had my car, but she also had a new Monte Carlo Chevrolet.

In the apartment were so many things that we couldn't afford—; expensive furniture and much more. She didn't try to hide anything.

I had seen enough, but before I left I took back the power of attorney given to her a year earlier and burned it. I told her that if she wanted to save our marriage, she and the girls could join me in Germany. She said she would let me know.

I left Louisiana without spending the night and headed east to Alabama and Georgia.

My father had remarried and built a small house in Anniston, Alabama. I hadn't seen him in many, many years, but I wanted to get to know him if I could. His wife was a big woman and not very good looking. Her name was Lois, and it was her personality, not her looks that I didn't like very much. I don't think she liked me either, but we were cordial and tried to get along. I learned that he had been with her in Memphis the whole time that I was there looking for him so many years ago. I didn't think about Memphis much anymore, but sometimes I would think about Sam and wonder about that very kind black man who had taken pity on a lost and confused white boy.

I left my father's house and went on to Macon to pay a short visit to my sister, Betty, and her husband, Mac, before going to Charleston, South Carolina, to board a plane to Germany.

When I arrived in Frankfurt, Germany, this time it was almost like coming home. I had a working knowledge of the German people and their language as well as the country itself.

My new assignment was Lindsey Air Force Station in downtown Wiesbaden. Lindsey had no aircraft and was an administrative headquarters.

My room was in an old World War II SS barracks within walking distance of my telephone shop, the NCO club, mess hall, and base exchange.

After meeting my new commanding officer, a lieutenant colonel who didn't seem like a very happy man, I processed in and went to meet the guys with whom I would be working.

One of the guys, a master sergeant, invited me to his home to meet his wife and kids and have a couple of beers.

After a few beers I asked to use the bathroom. I didn't see any humor in using the bathroom but the sergeant and his wife seemed amused. I soon found out why. While standing there relieving myself I caught a glimpse out of the corner of my eye of something moving. I turned my head slightly, and there, crawling along the base of the wall, was a six-foot-long python. I shouted, "Oh, shit!" and hosed down the wall while zipping up as I ran out of the bathroom. That was the first time I ever pissed on and got pissed off at the same time. I damned near had a heart attack! The sergeant said, "I see you met our pet, Pete," and he laughed like hell. I didn't think it was funny at all, and I never went back to his house.

A Volkswagen dealership was just outside the gate, so I went there and bought a new Volkswagen. I had learned a long time ago that if I wanted to travel and see Europe, I had to have a car. So now I had one.

The Eagle's Club at Lindsey was a very nice NCO club. It was a four-story building with a stag bar and pool tables in the basement, main bar and snack bar on the first level, a ballroom and two bars with a full-time piano player at one, and a four-star restaurant on the top floor.

Having a conversation with a couple of guys one night at the club, I discovered one of them was a member of a dive group that was exploring the lakes in the region looking for airplanes that had been shot down during the war. After learning of my experience, they asked me to join them. I still had my regulator mask and snorkel but no wet suit or tank. I went to a local scuba store and purchased both.

We started our search on a mountain lake by cutting a hole in the ice and using a long quarter-inch lifeline. We would go in a circle, get out, cut another hole, and repeat the process, working our way around the lake. While we dove we would leave the engines running in the cars with heaters on so we wouldn't freeze after getting out of our wet suits. We also had thermos jugs filled with GLO wine, a hot mixture of wine, honey, and lemon juice. That stuff would warm you up in a hurry! We never did find the rumored downed fighters, but we had a lot of fun, especially after the dive and the hot wine.

One night I went barhopping in Wiesbaden, and driving down a very narrow cobblestoned street (more like an alley) a group of eight or ten young Germans about nineteen to twenty-one tried to stop my car by standing in front of me and blocking the street. There was no way I was going to stop and let them pull me out of my car and beat the hell out of me, so I did what I had to do to get out of the situation. I dropped down to first gear and ran over their asses. My car jumped and thumped as I ran over a couple of them, and I never looked back. Once I got back to Lindsey I parked my car in a good hiding spot and stayed on base for about three weeks. I never heard anything about it, so I don't suppose I hurt or killed anyone. They will probably think twice before trying to stop another GI, though.

While I was at Wiesbaden I had a unique opportunity for a rare experience. As an apprentice Mason I had never been given the chance to be elevated to a higher degree because of my assignments. In Wiesbaden I went to a German Masonic Blue Lodge and had a Mason work with me until I was ready to try and be raised to master Mason. I finally passed the test and was raised at Lodge 838 in Wiesbaden, Germany. Wow! What an experience that was.

Summer came, and one day at the telephone shop a clerk from our orderly room came in and said, "Sergeant Russell, the colonel wants to see you right now." So I hotfooted over to the colonel's office, and when I looked through his door, I saw two very sharp German police officers talking with the old man. I thought about those guys I had run over and said to myself, "I'm going to prison for sure!" My heart was pounding when I saluted and reported to the colonel. He introduced me to the police officers and said, "Sergeant Russell, these gentlemen need your help." I said, "Sure, I'll help if I can."

It seemed that the local police rescue divers were spread very thin, and they wanted an experienced diver to help in the recovery of a teenager who disappeared in a nearby lake. I don't know who told the colonel about my diving qualifications, but I went to my barracks, got my gear, and followed the cops.

The lake was at an exclusive resort and country club with mostly wealthy members. I went out to the area on a boat with the kid's parents and some club officials and started my search. The water was only fifteen or twenty feet deep but with zero visibility. I had to feel my way with my hands, and after about an hour I found the seventeen-year-old boy. I had recovered drowning victims before, and they were always the same—facedown, backs of their hands on the bottom, and elbows up. When I got the boy up, the couple in the boat put a blanket over me and gave me some cognac. It wasn't until then that I discovered they were his parents. It was very sad.

The club officials gave me a membership card and said I could come back anytime as an honorary member. I never went back, though, because I just couldn't take advantage of a situation like that. I did offer my assistance to the local police, though, if they ever needed me again.

I wrote Beth and told her that I needed to know her intentions. I could not and would not continue our marriage like this. I waited for an answer.

I've always liked to work with kids and decided to get involved with Little League again, but this time as a coach. Two or three weeks after joining the Little League coaching staff we had a big game at Bremerhaven, a port city in the north of Germany about 250 miles away. It was a playoff game between the air force kids at Bremerhaven and Wiesbaden.

I was acting as first base coach during the game, and about midway through the game time was called, and one of the umpires came out and said, "You've got to go back to Lindsey right away. You have an emergency telegram." I couldn't imagine who would send me a telegram, so I jumped in my Volkswagen and drove back to Lindsey. It was on a Sunday, so I had to get the telegram from the OD (officer of the day).

The telegram was from Beth, and she said if I wanted to see the kids again, I had better come and get them because she would no longer take care of them; she was turning them over to me.

The next morning I went to the commander and let him see the telegram. I asked him for a humanitarian reassignment, but he turned my request down. I said, "Do I have permission to go over your head, sir?" He said, "You do not."

I went directly over to the Western Union office at Lindsey and sent a telegram to Senator Richard B. Russell, chairman of the Armed Services Committee, and explained my situation and told him that my commander had denied my request for a humanitarian reassignment. The next day I got orders for reassignment to Maxwell Air Force Base. Senator Russell was from Georgia, and the fourth most powerful man in Washington. My name being Russell and also from Georgia didn't hurt. I got a letter from him inviting me to visit him in Washington if I had the opportunity. I'm sure that was a gesture of kindness, but I didn't accept his invitation to go by his office. However, I did write a letter thanking him for his help.

When I signed out at Lindsey, the colonel was fuming, but he didn't dare say anything. He didn't know what my

RETURN TO ALABAMA

Back at Maxwell it was almost as though I had never left. The communications squadron was in the same building, the telephone shop was still where it was before, and almost everything else was the same. Déjà vu!

The base housing office gave me a two-bedroom house with a fenced-in back yard, and living room, dining room, and bedroom furniture. They even gave me cooking utensils and plates with all I needed to start keeping house.

Now I needed transportation, so I went into Montgomery and bought a new Plymouth.

Next I went to Louisiana to pick up the kids. They were with a family that Beth had left them with until I picked them up. I loaded up their clothes and toys and headed back to Alabama. The next few months were going to be the most stressful time of my life.

I enrolled the five-year-old in kindergarten and the two-year-old in daycare; every morning I got up, fixed breakfast, and dressed them for school. Brushing their hair, doing pigtails or ponytails with little bows, and doing the things that little girls needed done was a new and trying experience for me. I still had my military duties to perform, and that required an overnight sitter at times.

This went on for about six months, and one day I got a call from Beth to bring her babies back to her. She wanted them back and promised not to give me anymore trouble. I would miss the bubble baths and laughter, bedtime stories and hugs from those beautiful little girls. They were happy with me, and I'm sure I spoiled them at times.

My friend Dan was going to Barksdale Air Force Base to stay overnight and then return to Maxwell. He asked if I would like to ride with him and share the cost of gas. Barksdale was at Bossier City, Louisiana, where I was going, so I accepted his offer.

Beth's apartment was about twenty miles from Barksdale, and Dan dropped me off and went back there. I had no intention of staying overnight at Beth's house because I really couldn't stand being around her anyway. We had a very heated discussion.

I went to the door and told her I was leaving. She said she would drive me to town, and I told her I'd walk. Before I closed the door behind me, I told her I wanted a divorce. The long walk back to town gave me time to cool off and shake away some of the anger and the hurt that I felt. It was over.

When Dan and I got back to Maxwell my life would slowly return to normal. I got rid of the house and moved into a room at the barracks. I wanted to get involved in scuba diving again, so I visited a local dive shop in Montgomery to get information on clubs in the area. The owner of the shop was a big, friendly guy named Burt. He and I had a lot in common. We were both experienced scuba instructors, and we were both pilots. Burt and I would eventually become very good friends.

Burt was teaching scuba classes three nights a week at the pool on base, and he asked me to help him. After I started helping him out with his classes I met some people that would also become good friends. One of my new friends was Doug, who was a very funny guy, a gourmet cook, a meticulous housekeeper, and smart. He was a civilian government employee.

After going on a few weekend dive trips to Florida with Burt and the newly certified divers, Doug asked me if I would like to move out of the barracks and share an apartment with him. After thinking about it for a while I moved to the apartment. Doug and I made the place into a very posh bachelors' pad. We were both neat freaks, and we shared the expenses down the middle.

On one of our trips to Florida, a local diver told us about a small crystal-clear pond near Ebro, Florida, that we might want to explore. We drove to Ebro and located the pond and saw a rush of water coming up in the middle of the pond. Burt and I put on our gear and went down about twenty feet to see where the water was coming form. The water was so clear that we could see about a hundred feet. We discovered a hole about three feet wide with a powerful flow of water gushing out.

We decided to organize an exploration dive and come back the following weekend and go into the hole to see what we could find.

We decided on two teams of two divers per team with eighty cubic feet of air in each of the twin tanks. A normal scuba tank is seventy-two cubic feet, so having 160 cubic feet of air would give us a real margin of safety. Next was a reel of quarter-inch nylon lifeline two hundred feet long. Burt and I would be the lead team, going in with the lifeline.. The safety team was an air force lieutenant named Talley, and Doug. Talley's job was to tie the end of the lifeline to a tree root or trunk, and then he and Doug would go in and stop at a knot in the rope that was half the length or about a hundred feet. They also carried an extra tank and waited at their assigned halfway spot for added protection. Were we safe?

It was extremely difficult getting past the strong current and into the hole, but once inside there was no pressure at all. So Burt and I took the reel and started our venture into the cave, letting the reel pay out the line as we slowly proceeded into the cave. There were stalactites and stalagmites all along the way, which indicated that the cave was once dry. There were also artifacts and old broken pottery of some long-gone inhabitants. The cave had tributaries leading off from the main cave. We could see quite a distance with our lights, but we kept to the main cave until our reel of lifeline came to its end.

We turned around to start back and discovered that our air bubbles had knocked silt loose from the cave ceiling and clouded up the water so badly that we couldn't see a damn thing. Thank God for the lifeline! We followed it until we reached our safety team. Talley was holding the end of the line, which had come untied and followed us in until it caught up to him and Doug. When they realized what had happened, someone panicked, and I caught a kicking flipper in my face that knocked my mask to one side, filling it with water. By the time I cleared my mask and shined my light around, everyone was out of sight. I couldn't find my way out because visibility was only about two feet. I still had about a hundred feet to the entry hole, so I decided to sit along the wall of the cave and see if the water would clear up a little. It wasn't happening, so I decided to curl myself into a ball and see if I could drift with the current. The thought entered my mind that what if I drifted into an underground river? I would be history! Nothing but a memory! So I drifted for what seemed like a very long time but probably wasn't. Finally I saw a very faint light that kept getting brighter and brighter until I shot out of the hole like a cannonball, ripping my wet suit against the jagged rocks.

I came up cussing and yelling about Talley's stupidity in not tying the line properly instead of just looping it around a stump. Burt was already out, and pretty soon Doug and Talley popped out. We could have been killed from Talley's carelessness. Burt was swearing about as much as I was, but I think I was the champion in the swearing category! Doug used to call me "silver tongue" when I got mad.

One thing is for sure. I'll never go cave diving again! I've been claustrophobic ever since.

None of the local dive clubs wanted wives or girlfriends to go on weekend dive trips with their men, so a group of us got together and formed our own club that welcomed the girls on our trips. The club was called the Dixie Divers and would eventually become one of the largest clubs in the Southeast. I was honored to be the first president of the club, but that didn't last long because I would go overseas again without the chance of seeing the club grow.

I must have gotten the message across to Beth because my divorce arrived by certified mail, and at last the nightmare was over, and I was officially a single man again. I was also a lot wiser.

My friend Dan was the head bartender at the NCO club, and I asked him for a job, and he hired me. Now I was my old self again, keeping busy as much as possible when I wasn't on duty at my air force job.

I also joined the Aero Club and started studying for my commercial pilot's license and instrument rating.

One of the regulars at the bar, a sergeant who I got to know quite well, was about to retire. His name was Wilson, and he had a little home with about five acres near the base. His story was tragic and about the saddest that I've ever heard, but true.

He told me that he decided to plant tomatoes on his property and sell them to wholesalers in the area.

He stopped by for his daily beer one day, and I asked him whatever happened to his tomato business. He explained that he couldn't find a buyer and had to plow the rotted tomatoes under. He said, "That's okay, though, because I'm going to raise quails for the area hunting preserve." He had purchased an incubator and some quail eggs through *Field & Stream* magazine. He put chicken wire around some of the property and even enclosed the top with chicken wire too.

Well, the eggs started hatching and all but one baby quail chick died from the two dozen eggs in the incubator. The chick was about the size of the end of your thumb. Wilson sent his son down to a nearby feed mill to get a handful of starter mash, a food used to feed baby chickens. He came back with twenty-five pounds, enough to feed a flock of chickens. His son was chasing the chick to feed him, and the chick stopped, but his son didn't! The chick was squashed by his son's number ten shoe!

He said, "To hell with that," and since he had a male and female miniature schnauzer he would breed dogs and sell the pups.

While he was waiting for the new pups he bought a couple of small motorcycles for him and his wife so they could ride around enjoying the countryside. When they reached a railroad crossing and were trying to go around the lowered gate, his wife was hit by a train and killed, a very heart-wrenching story.

A couple of months later he came into the bar while I was

working and asked me to stop by his house and have a beer with him. He wanted to talk about something.

When I went over to his place, dogs and puppies were running all over the place. The doggie door that he had installed was flapping back and forth nonstop. He said he loved the puppies so much that he couldn't bear selling them.

We sat down and opened beers, and he wanted my opinion on what he was about to do. He said, "Air America wants men to ride (shotgun) as gunners on courier flights in and out of Laos." The pay was high, and it was tax-free.

I said, "What good is the money if you're dead? Air America (the CIA) loses guys all the time; you just don't hear about it." Well, he signed up anyway, and I never heard from him again. Too bad.

One day when I was flying, I heard a female voice on the Maxwell air traffic control frequency. I had never heard a female voice in the tower, and since I was authorized in the tower I decided to check it out. I looked her over, but she didn't know it. A pretty redhead was a big improvement in the tower.

I met her at the club one day when she was campaigning for the WAF's charity ball. Each of the candidates for charity ball queen was collecting dollars for votes.

Sharon Daly (Rusty) was selling kisses for votes, and I gave her a vote, and she gave me a kiss, and then I went back and stood in line again.

Rusty would later become my wife and the mother of my two sons.

One day I took her on a flight to Milledgeville to visit my old friend Frank. She was a qualified air traffic controller with a good FAA rating and understood what I was doing on the flight.

We were flying under instrument conditions because visibility was extremely poor. Although I had instrument training, I wasn't yet instrument rated. About thirty miles outside of Milledgeville I radioed the airport but didn't get a reply. I called another FAA facility to assure that my radio was working, and when I found out that it was, I continued on and started my descent until I saw the Milledgeville runway right in front of my nose.

When we landed I found out the airport radio could receive but not transmit. They fixed it after I landed.

The next day, after leaving Frank and his wife, Jane, we had a pleasant and uneventful flight back to Montgomery. That was the first time Rusty ever flew with me.

A couple of months later I got orders for my last overseas assignment, Thailand.

I left my car with Rusty because I would be coming back to Maxwell to process out of the air force for my retirement.

I said good-bye to Rusty and was off again to a one-year assignment overseas.

THAILAND

Crossing the Pacific Ocean was getting to be a habit. This time we stopped at Wake Island, and then it was on to Bangkok. We stayed in Bangkok a couple of days, then got on a C-130 for our final leg of the trip to Udorn, Thailand. Udorn was close to the Laos border in the Northeast part of Thailand, where around-the-clock flights to Vietnam were conducted.

I was assigned to the 621st Tactical Control Squadron, which I would call home for the next year. My barracks was a two-story building constructed of teakwood with a continuous window running the length of the barracks and screened in on both sides. The mosquitoes were a real problem, so every bunk was equipped with a mosquito net enclosure. It was always hot and humid, with the temperature soaring to well over a hundred degrees at midday when the sun beat down on the metal roof. Ceiling fans helped a lot, but it wasn't enough.

The small town of Udorn was about two miles from the base

and was comprised of all kinds of shops selling precious stones, gold, ivory carvings, and even stuffed cobras. Anything you wanted you could find in Udorn, and, of course, there were the bars and the usual camp followers.

Just outside the gate was a small village with more bars and a lot of thatched-roof structures.

Once I went to work my primary job was as a training NCO with the responsibility of training the royal Thai Air Force in telecommunications equipment and operation. I found that they had to be trained over and over again on the same subject. Sometimes I thought their retention was about thirty minutes, and at times I felt like slapping them in the head with a clipboard just to keep their attention. But, in all honesty, the problem was the language barrier. I liked the little guys, though. They were all very friendly with an ever-present smile.

Among the many things that the Tactical Control Squadron did in the Vietnam War effort was to certify infrared films taken from gunships attacking the Ho Chi Minh Trail at night. The films were on sound tracks between the gunners and the pilots, and they were awesome, to say the least. My squadron picked them up daily, reviewed them, and sent them to the White House. I had the privilege of reviewing some of these top-secret films before they were dispatched.

We also had a detachment stationed at Monkey Mountain in Vietnam, an intelligence-gathering outpost. I went there a couple of times, but I didn't mind. Anytime you went over Vietnam airspace within a given month, you got one month's hazardous duty pay. It wasn't much, but it was something.

I had a friend, Master Sergeant Smith, a small, trim, blond-headed guy, who was meaner than a snake when he had a little too much to drink. He was one of my best friends in Thailand, and I liked him a lot. I guess the reason we got along so well was that we would always say it like it was. It didn't matter if it was to an officer or not. He respected my guts, and I respected his.

One time Smitty caught a stomach virus the medics called "the lettuce bug." It could be deadly if not treated, and you couldn't hold anything down that you ate. Smitty lost a lot of weight in the hospital, and he was already small. I went to visit him one day, and before I went into his room I asked the doctor how he was doing. The doctor told me he was improving and would have the bug whipped in no time.

I went in, and when he saw me, he gave me a big grin, and I said, "Damn, Smitty you look terrible I think you're gonna die!" He said, "Thanks, Russ, you son of a bitch!" He liked mystery novels, and before I left I gave him one I had picked up at the exchange. I had taken a razor blade and very carefully cut out the last page so he couldn't see how the story ended.

Another time Smitty and I went to the little village outside the base and started barhopping. Walking down the street we came upon a balloon vender with a big bunch of helium-filled balloons. We bought the whole bunch of maybe twenty-five balloons. We then rolled up an old newspaper and tied it to the balloon string. Setting one end of the paper on fire, we let it go. Soaring into the night sky, the flame kept getting bigger and bigger until it reached the helium "bombs," and then there was a big explosion. Pieces of burning paper started falling earthward toward all those thatched roofs in the village. Smitty and I got the hell out of there. It was a stupid thing to do. It must have been Smitty's idea!

An empty metal building was next to my barracks, and there were no plans to use it for anything. My commander was a colonel, and one day I asked him if I could make it into a little club for the guys in our squadron. After some questions and answers I assured him there would be no hard liquor in the club, only beer, snacks, and card tables. He gave me a thumbs-up, and the project got under way.

We needed leatherette and Formica for the bar, fireproof wall coverings and all kinds of stuff that we could pick up in Udorn. I passed the hat around and assured anyone who refused to drop a buck in the hat that he would get his ass kicked! We built the bar and used foam rubber to pad the bar, which we appropriated from some navy aircraft. We also acquired a two-ton air conditioner from the navy.

When we completed the "621st Little Club" and hired a Thai girl to bartend and serve hotdogs and other goodies, we had a formal grand opening with the colonel cutting the ribbon. Some of the guys called it Russ's club, but it wasn't. I just had the brainstorm and got it started, that's all.

Rusty had written me and said she could call me on a military line if I had a phone. So again I went to the commander and got permission to install a phone in my hooch (barracks).

I put the wall phone on one of the support posts near my bunk and gave Rusty the number.

A few days later my house girl (her name was Song) came running into the little club yelling, "Sargi, Sargi, you come quick! You have telephone!" The phone was on the cradle where she had hung up. She was yelling, "You talk, Sargi, you talk! I showed her and explained that she couldn't hang up the phone. I said, "Song, when the phone rings again, put it on the floor and run and find me." She said, "Okay, Sargi!"

About an hour later Song came running in shouting "Sargi, Sargi, you have telephone!" I ran to my hooch, and this time it was on the floor. I picked it up and said, "Hello, this is Sergeant Russell." The voice on the other end said, "Who was that bitch?!" It seemed that Rusty had been trying to get through for hours and just happened to get my little house girl, who had never seen a phone in her life.

I had a little Thai friend named "Joe." I never did know his Thai name, so I just called him Little Joe. He was a professional kickboxer and was the nicest little guy you would ever meet. I watched him fight several times, and he was really good.

A leper colony was about thirty miles from the base, and sometimes I would go there on weekends to help the missionaries with their projects and to bring them stuff from the base exchange, such as toiletries and hard-to-get items, especially for the ladies. They were really wonderful people to do the selfless work they were doing. I admired them tremendously.

I tried to get Little Joe to go with me on several occasions, but he was afraid of the lepers.

I had another good friend who was a captain, and he and I were buddies. Sometimes I would sneak him into the NCO club, and he would sneak me into the officers' club. His name was Jack, a little older than me with a balding head. I told him I was going to get him in trouble if he kept hanging around with me. He tried to get me to stop cussing so much, but, being a sergeant, I think it was my duty, wasn't it?

We had an outdoor theater, and we would hide a bottle of rum and sneak it in. During the playing of the national anthem they would project the flag on the screen, revealing about twenty-five or thirty lizards. We would make bets on how many would be on the screen. The guy who would miss the actual count by the widest margin would have to get the cokes for our rum all during the movie. When it rained, we would just sit there and enjoy the cool rain on our hot, sweaty bodies.

It was so hot and humid that a cool shower before sacking out was a must in order to be comfortable. The showers were in a separate building, and at night you had to take a flashlight and look for cobras before taking a shower, a constant danger in Thailand.

When my time was nearly up, and I was getting ready to go back to the States for retirement, the colonel dropped in to have a beer with the guys. I had been letting my sideburns grow out because when I got out of the air force, I wanted to look like a civilian.

While standing there having a beer with the colonel, the sergeant major walked up and said, "Sergeant Russell, get those sideburns cut off." I said, "Why don't you try and cut them off, Sarge?" He turned beet red and the colonel said, "Leave Sergeant Russell alone; he's going home in a few days for retirement." The sergeant major walked away. I guess I was kind of a loose cannon at times. I had been that way since my army days. I just didn't let anyone push me around.

The colonel gave me a going-away dinner the night before I left Thailand. At my place setting was a bottle of Chivas Royal Salute, a gift from the colonel. The colonel got up to say a few words, but first he said, "If anybody touches Sergeant Russell's Royal Salute they will answer to me." Then he said, "If anyone in the air force deserves to be a senior noncommissioned officer, it's Sergeant Russell. You've been dealt a bad hand by the system, and the air force owes you a lot." Those words meant a lot coming from him.

Thailand 1971 just before retiring (age 37)

Retirement

All my friends and my house girl, Song, came to see me off at the Udorn Terminal.

Song had kept my hooch clean and done my laundry for the past year. She was like a happy little girl, and she had a husband who was a master sergeant in the Royal Thai Air Force. They lived in a small jungle village not too far from the base, and they took me there for a going-away party, Thai style, a few days before I was to leave.

She was emotional as she placed a lei of flowers around my neck and said, "Oh, Sargi, why I love you so much?" With tears in her eyes she put her palms together under her chin and said in a soft voice, "Lah Gorn," which means in Thai, "Good-bye."

So I said good-bye to Song and my friends Jack, Smitty, and a bunch of guys from my squadron, and with mixed emotions I climbed aboard the C-130 that would take me to Bangkok for my flight to the States.

I took with me two dress uniforms and the fatigue uniform I was wearing. When I got to the hotel in Bangkok where I would stay overnight waiting to catch my plane to San Francisco, I would trash my fatigues and put on one of my dress uniforms for the trip home—the last dress uniform I would use for my retirement ceremony at Maxwell. As I used the military clothes, I would throw them in the trash, put on civilian clothes and never look back.

I had seen too many guys dwell on leaving the military and turn to the bottle in self-pity. That wasn't about to happen to me. I would take my retirement, divorce the air force, and move on with my life. The only thing I would keep would be my memories.

At the hotel bar in Bangkok I started talking to a couple of civilian executives that worked for ITT. They asked if I was stationed in Bangkok, and I explained that I was on my way back to the States to retire from twenty years in the military. They asked me what I did in the air force, and I said I was a telephone technician. They got all excited and offered me a job with ITT. I said, "Thanks, but I have to go back to the States for my retirement." The guy who seemed to be the boss said, "We will pay your way back to either Bangkok or Singapore, Malaysia, give you a great salary, monthly living allowance, and thirty days vacation each year, all tax-free." I was flattered but turned down the offer.

I had seriously considered going to Australia after I retired and even sent for immigration application forms from the Australian consulate general. But being the patriot that I am, I forgot the idea of becoming an Australian.

I had spent almost half my life overseas, and it was time to go home and stay put.

I boarded the American Air Lines plane the next morning for the long flight home and, as I learned a long time ago, found a seat in the far rear of the plane. I could stand up and move around without bothering anyone, talk to the stewardesses, and the coffee was right there. It was much better than sitting in one spot for twelve hours. This would be my tenth time crossing the Pacific Ocean and probably my last. I had crossed the Atlantic Ocean six times too.

I got a commercial flight from San Francisco to Montgomery, Alabama. When I came down the steps off the plane, Rusty was waiting for me.

She had my car, which I let her use while I was away, but I let her drive because I hadn't been behind the wheel in over a year and wasn't quite ready for the traffic.

The next day I processed through personnel at Maxwell and was asked if I wanted a parade for my retirement ceremony; I declined. I had been in over a hundred parades and had listened to guys complain and swear at the guys the parade was being held for, and I wasn't about to be one of those bad guys. Those hundreds of guys sweating on the parade ground didn't know who the hell I was anyway and didn't give a damn. So much for parades.

I took a ninety-day terminal leave that would give me time to get my feet on the ground and decide what to do with the rest of my life.

One of the first things I did was to trade in my Plymouth for a new Oldsmobile Cutlass Supreme. It was a beautiful car with all the creature features I wanted.

I had always wanted to live in central Florida, so Rusty and I went to Winter Park and got a townhouse next to a pool that we used every day. The mailman even brought my mail to the pool.

One day at the pool I met a guy by the name of Art. He was the regional manager for Litton, a telephone company owned by Litton Industries. When he discovered that I was a telephone technician, he offered me a job as a contract installer working with United Telephone Company in Fort Meyers, Florida. I accepted and would go to work after Rusty and I were married on.

My official retirement from the air force was after my ninety-day terminal leave was over on the first of October.

A New Beginning

Rusty and I were married in Farmington, Michigan, on the ninth of October, 1971, nine days after my official retirement from the air force.

Her mother, Marilyn; brother, Mike; aunt and uncle; cousins; and grandparents all accepted me into their family. It was like having a family for the first time. Even after all these years, it's still like that. I will always be grateful for my "new family."

We went back to Winter Park for a short while before beginning my first job as "Russ the civilian." My name had slowly changed over the years to Russ instead of Earl because in the military you are always referred to by your last name. Your buddies would always shorten it with a nickname, mine being Russ. Now everyone calls me Russ, even my family. I really should say my second job. I had taken a job as a door to door vacuum cleaner salesman that only lasted a couple of days.

I knocked on a door and was let in by a retired engineer and started my demonstration and sales pitch. The guy stopped me halfway through my demonstration and said, "What the hell are you doing? What did you do before trying to sell vacuum cleaners?" I explained that I had just retired from the air force and was a telephone technician. He said, "Well, you should stick to the telephone business. Put down that vac and go into the kitchen and get a beer and relax. You shouldn't be a door to door salesman because you suck at it!" So ended my career as a vacuum cleaner salesman.

Rusty and I went to Fort Meyers and rented an apartment that was located on the edge of a swamp. There was all kinds of wildlife, including alligators and palmetto bugs all over the place. In Florida they call them palmetto bugs, but they are nothing but giant cockroaches—disgusting things, to say the least.

After working for United Telephone Company a couple of weeks as a contractor I called in to my dispatcher to clear my completed work orders. My dispatcher, a lady named Muriel, said, "Russ what are you trying to prove?" I asked her what she meant, and she said, "You always complete all your work orders and are doing much more than the other installers." I said "Muriel, I'm the only contractor here, and I do what I'm supposed to do." She said, "Well, slow down; some of the guys are starting to complain that you're making them look bad." I told her I work the same pace that I was used to working in the air force, but I'd slow down and start spending more time in coffee shops if that would make everybody happy.

I had always heard that the military had it easy and only

worked half as hard as their counterparts in civilian jobs. That turned out to be a bunch of crap and was far from the truth. I found out that in the air force we worked twice as hard for half the pay. I didn't slow down much because I wasn't comfortable being a loafer. I am what I am, take it or leave it!

It wasn't long before Fort Meyers started getting to Rusty. There were too many old people and almost no younger people our age.

One day I called the regional manager, Art, and asked if I could get transferred. He said, "You want to go to the Midwest?" I asked where, and he said, "Detroit." I said, "Absolutely, I'll go; Rusty will love this!"

So I went to Detroit and teamed up with a guy named Bob. Our first job together was installing a big telephone system in a hotel in Grand Rapids. We didn't have an office and had to communicate by phone daily with the vice president of Litton in New York. Bob and I were floaters and worked all over the Midwest until Litton opened an office in Detroit, and I was reassigned as an installations supervisor, and Bob went to Columbus, Ohio.

Rusty and I bought our first house in Novi, a suburb of Detroit. While we lived there I enrolled in a commercial pilot's school and started training mostly in night flying. I hadn't flown as a pilot since leaving Maxwell a couple of years earlier. It felt good.

The economy was getting really bad, and thousands were out of work in Michigan. Litton closed its doors, so I took a job as installations manager with Lear Siegler, a competitor of Litton. A few months later that company also closed its doors.

I was offered a job with a company called Inn Management, with offices in Orlando and Tampa. I would manage its industrial warehouses and lease space to businesses. Inn Management Corporations was owned by the Holiday Inn Group, and soon after Rusty and I moved to Orlando and moved into our new house the company also closed its doors. Now I had a new house and no job. This was getting to be a habit.

After closing on our new house, our real estate agent, a very nice lady named Thelma, took us to lunch at a country club where she was a member. During lunch I told her I was unemployed as of a couple of days ago. I thought she was going to faint. She said, "My God, don't tell anyone you closed on a mortgage without having a job!" I told her not to worry, that I would get a job.

Rusty and I started drawing unemployment pay, as about half of America was doing at the time. We also enrolled in college on the GI Bill, and I had my military retirement pay. Financially we were okay, and even had enough to play golf every day after classes.

I tried several jobs until I finally got a call from a large telephone interconnect company located in Winter Park, just a short distance from our house.

I was hired as the installations supervisor covering the entire state of Florida, with offices in Winter Park, Miami,

Tampa, Jacksonville, and Tallahassee. I was always on the road going from job to job. I wasn't playing much golf anymore.

Rusty was pregnant with our first child, and the guys at the golf club designed a special club for her with the shaft of the club following the contour of her very pregnant stomach. If she had continued playing after the baby was born, they were going to design a special baby seat to attach to the golf cart.

A GROWING FAMILY

Kevin William Russell was born on January 28, 1976, at 7:12 p.m. at Florida Hospital in Orlando.

My heart swelled with pride with the birth of my first son. He was a beautiful, chubby baby and I called him heavy Kevie. The indescribable love I felt for him led me to find a job that would allow me to spend more time at home.

I went to the general manager of the telephone company and asked for a move into the sales department. I had saved many sales that salesmen had missold because of their lack of technical knowledge of the equipment. I liked dealing with people, and I knew I had more skill than most of the salespeople at our company. The manager turned me down and said no intercompany transfers were allowed.

I turned in my desk keys and car keys and went to work for ITT the following day as a salesman. Maybe it wasn't smart, but all I was thinking about was spending more time with my family. I always did have more guts than brains.

Earl Russell

Seventeen months after my first son was born, Jason Robert Russell was born on June 7, 1977, at 9:46 p.m. at Florida Hospital.

I was so proud I could hardly stand it. Jason grew into one of the most beautiful little boys I have ever seen. The two boys were totally different, but both were beautiful boys.

I was determined that they would never be neglected or feel the pain of despair that I felt as a boy.

We were very lucky when we moved into our new home in Orlando. On each side of us were two great families, Joe and Marianne and their two children, Mike and Lisa, on one side, and Rans and Sara, with their three kids, Cindy, Susan, and Young Rans, on the other side.

Eight-year-old Rans, the baseball superstar, christened our new house with a fastball through one of our windows. Nobody was upset except Little Rans, but he soon got over it when he discovered that his new neighbors weren't monsters and wouldn't eat him alive.

Over the years, Rans and Sara have become very close friends.

Return to Michigan

After the election of President Jimmy Carter the economy got so bad that businesses stopped buying telephone systems, and gasoline was so expensive that using a car for work was difficult.

I got a job offer from Tate Communications in the Detroit area, so it was back to Michigan again.

We bought a condo in Novi, and I reported to work with the new company. Rusty got a job at a nearby bank, and we settled in at our new home in Michigan.

The condo had an unfinished basement, so I went to work in my spare time and finished it off. It turned out to be a nice play area for the kids. Jason was just a little guy, and his big brother Kevin was about four years old.

One day the tornado warnings sounded, and the kids and I retreated to the basement for milk and cookies until the all-clear sounded on the sirens outside. Jason wanted to call his mother at the bank to let her know that everything was okay at home. When Rusty answered the phone, Jason shouted. "Momma, Momma, tomatoes are coming, tomatoes are coming!" Through the years we have told that story many times, and Jason is a little embarrassed each time we tell it.

Another time Rusty and I were busy doing little odds and ends and all of a sudden we didn't see Kevin anywhere. I checked upstairs and then the basement and still no Kevin. Then we noticed one of the screens was missing on a window. We looked out the open window, and Kevin was in the bushes below the window. The screen had popped out when he was looking out, and he fell through. After the panic subsided and Kevin was checked over from head to toe, we found him to be okay. It scared the hell out of us, though.

The condo was too small, and we sold it and moved into a much bigger home in a nice neighborhood with a school just down the street and kids just the right age for playmates for the boys. It was a big improvement, and the finishing off of the basement at the condo really paid off.

We went on vacation to St. Simons Island to play a little golf and play in the ocean with the boys. Of all times to get hurt, I pulled a muscle in my back, and the pain was so bad that I couldn't play golf at all. I guess I ruined the vacation for everyone.

We decided to cut the vacation short at the golf resort and visit our friends Rans and Sara, who had moved to Norcross, Georgia, near Atlanta.

While we were there Rusty and I started looking at model homes in the area. Rans and Sara's daughter, Susan, had turned into a beautiful young lady of about fifteen and acted as our guide.

Unknown to Rusty, I was doing some research on job opportunities in the Atlanta area.

After much consideration we decided to have a house built and relocate to Norcross. When the house was completed we moved, and I took a job with a telephone company in Atlanta.

NORCROSS, GEORGIA

Our new home had a giant oak tree in the backyard and some other trees that were just right for a tree house for the boys. I enlisted the help of Kevin and Jason, and we went to work on their tree house.

The boys started bringing things like plywood, nails, shingles, and carpet from all of the homes under construction in the neighborhood. The material the boys were gathering were remnants left over from the finished homes and discarded. I wasn't teaching my sons to steal.

When the project was finished the tree house was about six feet off the ground with stairs going up to a little porch, a door with a little see-through window, Plexiglas windows, and wall-to-wall carpet. It was a father and sons project that really turned out great.

One day the project superintendent came to me and said, "Mr. Russell, you have got to keep your boys off the roofs of my houses!" It seemed that Kevin, with his little brother tagging along, would go up onto the roofs from the dormer windows and sit there and watch the world go by. I'm sure it was great fun for the six- and four-year-old boys but very dangerous. I should have been watching them more closely. I was a very protective father and on several occasions when my boys were growing up, I stood nose to nose with some of the men in our subdivision and let them know exactly what I thought if I felt my boys were being threatened. I would stand up for the kids in the neighborhood too. I would not tolerate kids being mistreated.

After about a year of working with the telephone company I decided that I knew more about the business than the people I had been working for.

I obtained catalogs and pricing from telephone equipment suppliers. Then I made work sheets of different systems, wrote out proposals and got my friend Sara to help me with my first proposal. Then I got a list of prospects and a list of installations and service technicians. Now I was ready, so I incorporated as "Russell Communications Inc."(RCI).

The first presentation I made was to the owner of a building supply company. Mr. Lummus was a very nice older gentleman. When I finished my presentation, Mr. Lummus said, "Mr. Russell, why should I buy from you when another established company has shown me a similar system with very little difference in price?" I replied, "Mr. Lummus, how big was your company the first day you started business?" He said, "I get your point. I'll sign your contract, but you had better not let me down!"

Several years later and after about two thousand systems

were sold, Mr. Lummus called me at home one evening. He said, "Mr. Russell, I'm calling to let you know that I'm retiring and moving to Florida, but before I go I just want you to know that you didn't let me down." That phone call was a wonderful thing for him to do, and I'll never forget him.

One day driving down Peachtree Industrial Boulevard I saw a little sign being put up in the rain at the edge of the road. It read, "Future home of Blue Haven Pools." I made a U-turn and went to the existing location of Blue Haven Pools.

I asked to see the owner or president. The receptionist said, "I'll get the sales manger." I said, "No, I will only talk to the boss." A guy by the name of Tom came out and took me into his office. After some conversation I determined that he would need about a $12,000 or $15,000 system at his new building. I said, "Tom, I want you to come over to my house and price up a pool for me and tell me if I can put a top-of-the-line pool in my backyard.

When he came over he made his drawings and gave me a price; we went into the house and sat down with a drink. I said, "Tom, I'll make you a deal. If you buy a telephone system from me, I'll buy your pool." We made a deal, and the pool was installed.

I taught the boys to swim without ever putting my hands on them in the pool. I used the knowledge learned as a scuba instructor and quickly turned my boys into little fish. We had many happy times in the pool with family and friends. Tom was pleased with his telephone system, too.

I had built my company into a reputable sales and service company starting alone in my den and growing into a dozen employees and a small fleet of service trucks.

One day moving into a large office across the street from our old offices I bought a case of beer for the guys helping us move. Each time before grabbing something to carry across the street, I would take a sip of my beer, crimp the can, and put it in the windowsill. When I came back over for another load, I picked up my beer and it was empty. I opened another beer, crimped the can, and put it on the windowsill. I came back, and it was empty again! This happened several times until I noticed little Jason staggering around drunk as a skunk. Each time I put my beer down Jason thought it was okay to drink his dad's beer.

Business was going well, and I bought a four-seat Cessna 172. It was a safe and reliable family airplane. It was less expensive than renting every time I wanted to fly. I used the Cessna for a lot of business trips and weekend fun flying with the boys.

When my company was about twelve years old I had built my net worth into over $1 million. The competition was fierce, the economy was getting bad again, and I made some poor business decisions. I put all my eggs into one basket by committing to a single supplier who provided proprietary equipment, a very critical mistake.

The boys had finished high school, I was drinking far too much trying not to watch my business go under, and it was taking its toll on my marriage.

I couldn't stop the downward spiral of Russell Communications and eventually was forced into bankruptcy. It was painful, embarrassing, and downright stupid. I had enjoyed the best reputation in the business and was well known in the business throughout the United States. It was extremely hard to take. I couldn't face my friends and competitors.

In addition to the company bankruptcy, I also filed a personal bankruptcy under the repayment plan. I felt it was my moral obligation to pay back as much as possible to the people that had trusted me. I paid out a lot of money over five years and had to start all over again and build my life back from nothing.

Rusty and I separated, and the kids wanted to get an apartment together.

I helped the boys as much as I could with furniture from my share of our household belongings—pots and pans and just about everything they needed to start housekeeping. It was the most difficult thing I've ever tried to do.

After Rusty and I sold the house, got the kids moved into their apartment, and all the loose ends taken care of, I loaded up my car with my clothes and our family dog, Sam, and headed south. I spent about six months in middle Georgia near Robins Air Force Base, and then headed farther south.

I thought about going to Mexico but decided against that and instead took a job in St. Augustine with a company installing equipment for AOL and doing the regular telephone systems, sales, and service.

LIVING ON THE LAKE

I left Florida and found a very nice townhouse on Lake Sinclair in Milledgeville. I had a boat dock, and I bought a boat that I named the SS *Tadpole*.

I had left Milledgeville as a boy of fifteen and now I was back again as an old man of sixty-five. My days were spent playing golf and trying to locate old childhood friends. I was bored to death.

One day I saw an ad in the local paper that read: "Tired of playing golf, fishing, and your nagging wife? Want to make some money and work your own hours doing a fun job?" Come on in and talk with us. So I went to Macon and interviewed for the job.

The job was with a custom home builder, and they needed someone to run an office in Milledgeville. The job entailed meeting with prospective home buyers who wanted to build a custom home on their own property. They could work with our plans or, in most cases, their plans. I would find myself dissecting their plans and helping them redesign their dream home. It was fun, and over several years with the company I learned a lot about the house building business.

One evening while having dinner at a restaurant with my childhood best friend, Frank, I couldn't help but notice a very large lady at the next table. Believe it or not, she was flossing her damn teeth.

I called my boss the next morning and said, "I've got to get the hell out of Milledgeville." He let me go to McDonough and open an office on the south side of Atlanta—a lot closer to my boys.

McDonough

I moved into an apartment in McDonough and settled down at my new office there.

Because of my bankruptcy my credit had been destroyed. The road to restoring my credit had been difficult, but now that the court had discharged the bankruptcy my credit had been reestablished. The reason I filed a personal bankruptcy instead of liquidating our assets was to keep Rusty's credit clean. Each time I leased an apartment I was required to pay the entire lease term in advance. It was very hard, but now I'm okay and shopping for a house.

I found a three-bedroom house on a hill over looking a church just outside of McDonough. I had a little over two acres and made a pitching green so I could practice my golf short game.

My boss decided to close the office in McDonough after a couple of years and operate the entire business from one office in Macon. I didn't want to move to Macon, so I retired. It was about time anyway because I was seventy years old—an old man who was tired of moving.

My son Kevin decided to build a home on the north side of Atlanta in the community of Buford. I agreed to help him, so I sold my house in McDonough and moved into a one-bedroom apartment nearby.

Kevin and his wife, Hillary, had found a beautiful two-acre lot, and I got to work with subcontractors, county building permits, and all the things required to build a house. The building of the house took almost a year, and I stayed busy as the construction superintendent from early morning until night every day for the entire time it took to complete the house.

Kevin and Hillary wanted me to design an apartment in the basement and live there after the house was completed. The house is a little over five thousand square feet, and I used twelve hundred square feet for myself. I have one bedroom with a huge walk-in closet, custom kitchen, great room, dining area, computer room, laundry room, and a private deck. It's very nice, and I have no complaints. Kevin and Hillary have two beautiful little girls who live upstairs, and I'm lucky enough to see them almost every day.

Jason and Kendra also have a beautiful little girl, but they live a few miles away, and I can't see them as often. I wish I could.

I still have itchy feet because of my vagabond nature, but I'm too old to keep wandering, so I'll stay put. Am I happy?

No, but I'm content, and that's enough. After all, I'm with the people I love and the people who love me.

During the many years of my travels I had crossed the Atlantic Ocean six times and the Pacific Ocean ten times, and the Mediterranean Sea numerous times, as well as the Adriatic Sea, the Baltic Sea, the North Sea, the Yellow Sea, and the Sea of Japan. I have seen and done many things in many countries and on many islands of the Pacific Ocean. The only thing I have from all that are the memories.

It's time for me to stop chasing my tail. The journey is over.

Epilogue

I've never liked myself very much because I could have been a much better person and done so much more with my life. I could have gotten that college degree I've always wanted, and I could have been a much better provider for my family. I regret these shortcomings, but the biggest disappointment of all is never feeling the joy of hugging my mother.

It gives me a kick when I can make people laugh and feel a little happiness. Sometimes my sister calls me when she feels a little down, and it pleases me when I can cheer her up and make her laugh.

Someday when I'm in heaven, I hope I can make it a little brighter by making everyone smile, and maybe, just maybe, I can bring a little smile to the face of God! Wouldn't that be great?! Wow! Wouldn't that be great?!

A Portrait of Me

If my heart could guide my hands I'd paint
a portrait of this old man

Not an image that you can see but something
deep inside of me

I'll start by painting a little boy with youthful
exuberance and childish joy

Next I would paint an eager young man, who
will see the world as only he can

Last I would paint an ageing old man and show
his life if I possibly can

I've learned from happiness and I've learned
from strife, so I know mine is not a wasted life

Some day when I climb those heavenly stairs
I will think of my children and the children of
theirs

When I get closer to Heavens door, I will think
Of the future but I can paint no more

I've painted a picture perhaps you can see, it's
just a little portrait, a portrait of me